*Season
of Migration
to the North*

Season of Migration to the North

TAYEB SALIH

Translated from the Arabic by Denys Johnson-Davies

HEINEMANN

Heinemann
A division of Reed Elsevier Inc.
361 Hanover Street   Portsmouth, NH 03801-3912
Offices and agents throughout the world

ISBN 0-435-90066-8

Printed in the United States of America
10 09 08 07   VP   27 28 29

cf opening of HoD.

It was, gentlemen, after a long absence – seven years to be exact, during which time I was studying in Europe – that I returned to my people. I learnt much and much passed me by – but that's another story. The important thing is that I returned with a great yearning for my people in that small village at the bend of the Nile. For seven years I had longed for them, had dreamed of them, and it was an extraordinary moment when I at last found myself standing amongst them. They rejoiced at having me back and made a great fuss, and it was not long before I felt as though a piece of ice were melting inside of me, as though I were some frozen substance on which the sun had shone – that life warmth of the tribe which I had lost for a time in a land 'whose fishes die of the cold'. My ears had become used to their voices, my eyes grown accustomed to their forms. Because of having thought so much about them during my absence, something rather like fog rose up between them and me the first instant I saw them. But the fog cleared and I awoke, on the second day of my arrival, in my familiar bed in the room whose walls had witnessed the trivial incidents of my life in childhood and the onset of adolescence. I listened intently to the wind: that indeed was a sound well known to me, a sound which in our village possessed a merry whispering – the sound of the wind passing through palm trees is different from when it passes through fields of corn. I heard the cooing of the turtle-dove, and I looked through the window at the palm tree standing in the courtyard of our house and I knew that all was still well with life. I looked at its strong straight trunk, at its roots that strike down into the ground, at the green branches hanging down loosely over its top, and I experienced a feeling of assurance. I felt not like a storm-swept feather but like that palm tree, a being with a background, with roots, with a purpose.

My mother brought tea. My father, having finished his prayers and recitations from the Koran, came along. Then my sister and brothers came and we all sat down and drank tea and talked, as we have done ever since my eyes opened on life. Yes, life is good and the world as unchanged as ever.

Suddenly I recollected having seen a face I did not know among those who had been there to meet me. I asked about him, described him to them: a man of medium height, of around fifty or slightly older, his hair thick and going grey, beardless and with a moustache slightly smaller than those worn by men in the village; a handsome man.

'That would be Mustafa,' said my father.

Mustafa who? Was he one of the villagers who'd gone abroad and had now returned?

My father said that Mustafa was not a local man but a stranger who had come here five years ago, had bought himself a farm, built a house and married Mahmoud's daughter – a man who kept himself to himself and about whom not much was known.

2

I do not know what exactly aroused my curiosity but I remembered that the day of my arrival he was silent. Everyone had put questions to me and I to them. They had asked me about Europe. Were the people there like us or were they different? Was life expensive or cheap? What did people do in winter? They say that the women are unveiled and dance openly with men. 'Is it true,' Wad Rayyes asked me, 'that they don't marry but that a man lives with a woman in sin?'

As best I could I had answered their many questions. They were surprised when I told them that Europeans were, with minor differences, exactly like them, marrying and bringing up their children in accordance with principles and traditions, that they had good morals and were in general good people.

'Are there any farmers among them?' Mahjoub asked me.

'Yes, there are some farmers among them. They've got everything – workers and doctors and farmers and teachers, just like us.' I preferred not to say the rest that had come to my mind: that just like us they are born and die, and in the journey from the cradle to the grave they dream dreams some of which come true and some of which are frustrated; that they fear the unknown, search for love and seek contentment in wife and child; that some are strong and some are weak; that some have been given more than they deserve by life, while others have been deprived by it, but that the differences are narrowing and most of the weak are no longer weak. I did not say this to Mahjoub, though I wish I had done so, for he was intelligent; in my conceit I was afraid he would not understand.

Bint Majzoub laughed. 'We were afraid,' she said, 'you'd bring back with you an uncircumcised infidel for a wife.'

But Mustafa had said nothing. He had listened in silence, sometimes smiling; a smile which, I now remember, was mysterious, like someone talking to himself.

I forgot Mustafa after that, for I began to renew my relationship with people and things in the village. I was happy during those days, like a child that sees its face in the mirror for the first time. My mother never wearied of telling me of those who had died that I might go and pay my condolences and of those who had married that I might go and offer my congratulations, and thus I crossed the length and breadth of the village offering condolences and congratulations. One day I went to my favourite place at the foot of the tall acacia tree on the river bank. How many were the hours I had spent in my childhood under that tree, throwing stones into the river and dreaming, my imagination straying to far-off horizons! I would hear the groaning of the water-wheels on the river, the exchange of shouts between people in the fields, and the lowing of an ox or the braying of a donkey. Sometimes luck would be with me and a steamer would pass by, going up- or down-river. From my position under the tree I saw the village slowly undergo a change: the water-wheels disappeared to be replaced on the bank of the Nile by pumps, each one doing the work of a hundred water-wheels. I saw the bank retreating year

4

after year in front of the thrustings of the water, while on another part it was the water that retreated. Sometimes strange thoughts would come to my mind. Seeing the bank contracting at one place and expanding at another, I would think that such was life: with a hand it gives, with the other it takes. Perhaps, though, it was later that I realized this. In any case I now realize this maxim, but with my mind only, for the muscles under my skin are supple and compliant and my heart is optimistic. I want to take my rightful share of life by force, I want to give lavishly, I want love to flow from my heart, to ripen and bear fruit. There are many horizons that must be visited, fruit that must be plucked, books read, and white pages in the scrolls of life to be inscribed with vivid sentences in a bold hand. I looked at the river – its waters had begun to take on a cloudy look with the alluvial mud brought down by the rains that must have poured in torrents on the hills of Ethiopia – and at the men with their bodies leaning against the ploughs or bent over their hoes, and my eyes take in fields flat as the palm of a hand, right up to the edge of the desert where the houses stand. I hear a bird sing or a dog bark or the sound of an axe on wood – and I feel a sense of stability, I feel that I am important, that I am continuous and integral. No, I am not a stone thrown into the water but seed sown in a field. I go to my grandfather and he talks to me of life forty years ago, fifty years ago, even eighty, and my feeling of security is strengthened. I loved my grandfather and it seems that he was fond of me. Perhaps one of the reasons for my friendship with him was that ever since I was small stories of the past used to intrigue me, and my grandfather loved to reminisce. Whenever I went away I was afraid he would die in my absence. When overcome by yearning for my family I would see him in my dreams; I told him this and he laughed and said, 'When I was a young man a fortune-teller told me that if I were to pass the age when the Prophet died – that's to say sixty – I'd reach a hundred.' We worked out his age, he and I, and found he had about twelve more years to go.

My grandfather was talking to me of a tyrant who had ruled over the district in the days of the Turks. I do not know what it was that brought Mustafa to mind but suddenly I remembered him and said to myself that I'd ask my grandfather about him, for he was very knowledgeable about the genealogy of everyone in the village and even of people scattered up and down the river. But my grandfather shook his head and said that he knew nothing about him except that he was from the vicinity of Khartoum and that about five years ago he had come to the village and had bought some land. All of the inheritors of this land had, with the exception of one woman, gone away. The man had therefore tempted her with money and bought it from her. Then, four years ago, Mahmoud had given him one of his daughters in marriage.

'Which daughter?' I asked my grandfather.

'I think it was Hosna,' he said. Then he shook his head and said, 'That tribe doesn't mind to whom they marry their daughters.' However, he added, as though by way of apology, that Mustafa during his whole stay in the village had never done anything

6

which could cause offence, that he regularly attended the mosque for Friday prayers, and that he was 'always ready to give of his labour and his means in glad times and sad' – this was the way in which my grandfather expressed himself.

Two days later I was on my own reading in the early afternoon. My mother and sister were noisily chattering with some other women in the farthest part of the house, my father was asleep, and my brothers had gone out on some errand or other. I was therefore alone when I heard a faint cough coming from outside the house and on getting up I found it was Mustafa carrying a large water melon and a basketful of oranges. Perhaps he saw the surprise on my face.

'I hope I didn't wake you,' he said. 'I just thought I'd bring some of the first fruit from my field for you to try. I'd also like to get to know you. Noon is not the time for calling – forgive me.'

His excessive politeness was not lost on me, for the people of our village do not trouble themselves with expressions of courtesy – they enter upon a subject at one fell swoop, visit you at noon or evening, and don't trouble to apologize. I reciprocated his expressions of friendship, then tea was brought.

I scrutinized his face as he sat with bowed head. He was without doubt a handsome man, his forehead broad and generous, his eyebrows set well apart and forming crescent-moons above his eyes; his head with its thick greying hair was in perfect proportion to his neck and shoulders, while his nose was sharply-pointed but with hair sprouting from the nostrils. When he raised his face during the conversation and I looked at his mouth and eyes, I was aware of a strange combination of strength and weakness. His mouth was loose and his sleepy eyes gave his face a look more of beauty than of handsomeness. Though he spoke quietly his voice was clear and incisive. When his face was at rest it gained in strength; when he laughed weakness predominated. On looking at his arms I saw that they were strong, with prominent veins; his fingers none the less were long and elegant, and when one's glance reached them, after taking in his arms and hands, there was the sensation of having all of a sudden descended from a mountain into a valley.

I decided to let him speak, for he had not come at such a time of intense heat unless he had something important to say to me. Perhaps, on the other hand, he had been prompted to come out of pure goodwill. However, he cut across my conjectures by saying, 'You're most likely the only person in the village I haven't already had the good fortune of getting to know.' Why doesn't he discard this formal politeness, being as we are in a village where the men when roused to anger address one another as 'You son of a bitch'?

'I have heard a lot about you from your family and friends.'

No wonder, for I used to regard myself as the outstanding young man in the village.

phony

'They said you gained a high certificate – what do you call it? A doctorate?' What do you call it? he says to me. This did not please me for I had reckoned that the ten million inhabitants of the country had all heard of my achievement.

'They say you were remarkable from childhood.'

'Not at all.' Though I spoke thus, I had in those days, if the truth be told, a rather high opinion of myself.

'A doctorate – that's really something.'

Putting on an act of humility, I told him that the matter entailed no more than spending three years delving into the life of an obscure English poet.

I was furious – I won't disguise the fact from you – when the man laughed unashamedly and said: 'We have no need of poetry here. It would have been better if you'd studied agriculture, engineering or medicine.' Look at the way he says 'we' and does not include me, though he knows that this is my village and that it is he – not I – who is the stranger.

However, he smiled gently at me and I noticed how the weakness in his face prevailed over the strength and how his eyes really contained a feminine beauty.

'But we're farmers and think only of what concerns us,' he said with a smile. 'Knowledge, though, of whatsoever kind is necessary for the advancement of our country.'

I was silent for a while as numerous questions crowded into my head: Where was he from? Why had he settled in this village? What was he about? However, I preferred to bide my time.

He came to my aid and said: 'Life in this village is simple and gracious. The people are good and easy to get along with.'

'They speak highly of you,' I said to him. 'My grandfather says you're a most excellent person.'

At this he laughed, perhaps because he remembered some encounter he had had with my grandfather, and he appeared pleased at what I had said. 'Your grandfather – there's a man for you,' he said. 'There's a man – ninety years of age, erect, keen of eye and without a tooth missing in his head. He jumps nimbly on to his donkey, walks from his house to the mosque at dawn. Ah, there's a man for you.' He was sincere in what he said – and why not, seeing that my grandfather is a veritable miracle?

I feared that the man would slip away before I had found out anything about him – my curiosity reached such a pitch – and, without thinking, the question came to my tongue: 'Is it true you're from Khartoum?'

The man was slightly taken aback and I had the impression that a shadow of displeasure showed between his eyes. Nevertheless he quickly and skilfully regained his composure. 'From the outskirts of Khartoum in actual fact,' he said to me with a forced smile. 'Call it Khartoum.'

He was silent for a brief instant as though debating with himself whether he should keep quiet or say any more to me. Then I saw the mocking phantom of a smile hovering round his eyes exactly as I had seen it the first day.

'I was in business in Khartoum,' he said, looking me straight in the face. 'Then, for a number of reasons, I decided to change over to agriculture. All my life I've longed to settle down in this part of the country, for some unknown reason. I took the boat not knowing where I was bound for. When it put in at this village, I liked the look of it.

Something inside me told me that this was the place. And so, as you see, that's how it was. I was not disappointed either in the village or its people.' After a silence he got up, saying that he was off to the fields, and invited me to dinner at his house two days later.

'Your grandfather knows the secret,' he said to me with that mocking phantom still more in evidence round his eyes, as I escorted him to the door and he took his leave of me.

He did not, though, give me the chance of asking: 'What secret does my grandfather know? My grandfather has no secrets.' He went off with brisk, energetic step, his head inclined slightly to the left.

Dinner w/ Mustafa

When I went to dinner, I found Mahjoub there, together with the Omda, Sa'eed the shopkeeper, and my father. We dined without Mustafa saying anything of interest. As was his wont he listened more than he talked. When the conversation fell away and I found myself not greatly interested in it, I would look around me as though trying to find in the rooms and walls of the house the answer to the questions revolving in my head. It was, however, an ordinary house, neither better nor worse than those of the well-to-do in the village. Like the other houses it was divided into two parts: one for the women and the other containing the diwan or reception-room, for the men. To the right of the diwan I saw a rectangular room of red brick with green windows;

its roof was not the normal flat one but triangular like the back of an ox.

Mahjoub and I rose and left the rest. On the way I asked Mahjoub about Mustafa. He told me nothing new but said, 'Mustafa's a deep one.'

I spent two months happily enough in the village and several times chance brought Mustafa and me together. On one occasion I was invited to attend a meeting of the Agricultural Project Committee. It was Mahjoub, the President of the Committee and a childhood friend of mine, who invited me. When I entered, I found that Mustafa was a member of the Committee. They were looking into a matter concerning the distribution of water to the fields. It seemed that certain people, including some members of the Committee, were opening up the water to their fields before the time allocated to them. The discussion became heated and some of them began shouting at each other. Suddenly I saw Mustafa jump to his feet, at which the uproar died down and they listened to him with great respect. Mustafa said it was important that people should submit to the rules of the Project, otherwise things would get out of hand and chaos would reign; especially was it incumbent upon members of the Committee to set a good example, and that if they were to contravene the law they would be punished like anyone else. When he stopped speaking most members of the Committee nodded their heads in approval; those against whom his words had been directed kept silent.

There was not the slightest doubt that the man was of a different clay, that by rights he should have been President of the Committee; perhaps because he was not a local man they had not elected him.

About a week later something occurred that stunned me. Mahjoub had invited me to a drinking session and while we were sitting about chatting along came Mustafa to talk to Mahjoub about something to do with the Project. Mahjoub asked him to sit down, but he declined with apologies. When Mahjoub swore he would divorce if he did not, I once again saw the cloud of irritation wrinkle Mustafa's brows. However, he sat down and quickly regained his usual composure.

Mahjoub passed him a glass, at which he hesitated an instant before he took it and placed it beside him without drinking. Again Mahjoub swore the same oath and Mustafa drank. I knew Mahjoub to be impetuous and it occurred to me to stop him annoying the man, it being quite evident he did not at all wish to join the gathering. On second thoughts, though, I desisted. Mustafa drank the first glass with obvious distaste; he drank it quickly as though it were some unpleasant medicine. But when he came to the third glass he began to slow up and to sip the drink with pleasure, the tension disappeared from the corners of his mouth, and his eyes became even more dreamy and listless. The strength you were aware of in his head, brow and nose became dissolved in the weakness that flowed with the drink over his eyes and mouth. Mustafa drank a fourth glass and a fifth. He no longer needed any encouragement, but Mahjoub was in any case continuing to swear he would divorce if the other did not drink up. Mustafa sank down into the chair, stretched out his legs, and grasped the glass in both hands; his eyes gave me the impression of wandering in far-away horizons. Then, suddenly, I heard him reciting English poetry in a clear voice and with an impeccable accent. It was a poem which I later found in an anthology of poetry about the First World War and which goes as follows:

> *Those women of Flanders*
> *Await the lost,*
> *Await the lost who never will leave the harbour*
> *They await the lost whom the train never will bring.*
> *To the embrace of those women with dead faces,*
> *They await the lost, who lie dead in the trenches,*
> *the barricade and the mud,*
> *In the darkness of night,*
> *This is Charing Cross Station, the hour's past one,*
> *There was a faint light,*
> *There was a great pain.*

After that he gave a deep sigh, still holding the glass between his hands, his eyes wandering off into the horizon within himself.

I tell you that had the ground suddenly split open and revealed an afreet standing before me, his eyes shooting out flames, I would not have been more terrified. All of a sudden there came to me the ghastly, nightmarish feeling that we – the men grouped together in that room – were not a reality

14

but merely some illusion. Leaping up, I stood above the man and shouted at him: 'What's this you're saying? What's this you're saying?' He gave me an icy look – I don't know how to describe it, though it was perhaps a mixture of contempt and annoyance. Pushing me violently aside, he jumped to his feet and went out of the room with firm tread, his head held high as though he were something mechanical. Mahjoub, busy laughing with the rest of the people in the gathering, did not notice what had occurred.

On the next day I went to him in his field. I found him busy digging up the ground round a lemon tree. He was wearing dirty khaki shorts and a rough cotton shirt that came down to his knees; there were smudges of mud on his face. He greeted me as usual with great politeness and said, 'Some of the branches of this tree produce lemons, others oranges.'

'What an extraordinary thing!' I said, deliberately speaking in English.

He looked at me in astonishment and said, 'What?' When I repeated the phrase he laughed and said, 'Has your long stay in England made you forget Arabic or do you reckon we've become anglicized?'

'But last night,' I said to him, 'you recited poetry in English.'

His silence irritated me. 'It's clear you're someone other than the person you claim to be,' I said to him. 'Wouldn't it be better if you told me the truth?' He gave no sign of being affected by the threat implicit in my words but continued to dig round the tree.

'I don't know what I said or what I did last night,'

15

he said when he had finished digging, as he brushed the mud from his hands without looking at me. 'The words of a drunken man should not be taken too seriously. If I said anything, it was the ramblings of a sleep-talker or the ravings of someone in a fever. It had no significance. I am this person before you, as known to everyone in the village. I am nothing other than that – I have nothing to hide.'

I went home, my head buzzing with thoughts, convinced that some story lay behind Mustafa, something he did not want to divulge. Had my ears betrayed me the night before? The English poetry he had recited was real enough. I had neither been drunk, nor yet asleep. The image of him sitting in that chair, legs spread out and the glass held in both hands, was clear and unequivocal. Should I speak to my father? Should I tell Mahjoub? Perhaps the man had killed someone somewhere and had fled from prison? Perhaps he – but what secrets are there in this village? Perhaps he had lost his memory? It is said that some people are stricken by amnesia following an accident. Finally I decided to give him two or three days and if he did not provide me with the truth, then I would tackle him about it.

I did not have long to wait, for Mustafa came to see me that very same evening. On finding my father and brother with me, he said that he wanted to speak to me alone. I got up and we walked off together.

'Will you come to my house tomorrow evening?' he said to me. 'I'd like to talk to you.'

When I returned my father asked me, 'What's Mustafa want?' I told him he wanted me to explain a contract for the ownership of some land he had in Khartoum.

Just before sunset I went to him and found him alone, seated in front of a pot of tea. He offered me some but I refused for I was impatient to hear the story; he must surely have decided to tell the truth. He offered me a cigarette, which I accepted.

I scrutinized his face as he slowly blew out the smoke; it appeared calm and strong. I dismissed the idea that he was a killer – the use of violence leaves a mark on the face that the eye cannot miss. As for his having lost his memory, this was a possibility. Finally, as Mustafa began to talk, I saw the mocking phantom around his eyes, more distinct than ever before, something as perceptible as a flash of lightning.

'I shall say things to you I've said to no one before. I found no reason for doing so until now. I have decided to do so lest your imagination run away with you – since you have studied poetry.' He laughed so as to soften the edge of scorn that was evident in his voice.

'I was afraid you'd go and talk to the others, that you'd tell them I wasn't the man I claimed, which would – would cause a certain amount of embarrassment to them and to me. I thus have one request to make of you – that you promise me on your honour, that you swear to me, you won't divulge to a soul anything of what I'm going to tell you tonight.'

He gave me a searching look and I said to him: 'That depends upon what you say to me. How can I promise when I know nothing about you?'

'I swear to you,' he said, 'that nothing of what I shall tell you will affect my presence in this village. I'm a man in full possession of my faculties, peaceful, and wanting only good for this village and its people.'

I will not conceal from you the fact that I hesitated. But the moment was charged with potentialities and my curiosity was boundless. The long and short of it was that I promised on oath, at which Mustafa pushed a bundle of papers towards me, indicating that I should look at them. I opened a sheet of paper and found it to be his birth certificate: Mustafa Sa'eed, born in Khartoum 16 August 1898, father Sa'eed Othman (deceased), mother Fatima Abdussadek. After that I opened his passport: the name, date and place of birth were the same as in the birth certificate. The profession was given as 'Student'. The date of issue of the passport was 1916 in Cairo and it had been renewed in London in 1926. There was also another passport, a British one, issued in London in 1929. Turning over the pages, I found it was much stamped: French, German, Chinese and Danish. All this whetted my imagination in an extraordinary manner. I could not go on turning over the pages of the passport. Neither was I particularly interested in looking at the other papers. My face must have been charged with expectancy when I looked at him.

Mustafa went on blowing out smoke from his cigarette for a while. Then he said:

'It's a long story, but I won't tell you everything. Some details won't be of great interest to you, while others. . . . As you see, I was born in Khartoum and grew up without a father, he having died several months before I was born. He did none the less leave us something with which to meet our needs – he used to trade in camels. I had no brothers or sisters, so life was not difficult for my mother and me. When I think back, I see her clearly with her thin lips resolutely closed, with something on her face like a mask, I don't know – a thick mask, as though her face were the surface of the sea. Do you understand? It possessed not a single colour but a multitude, appearing and disappearing and intermingling. We had no relatives. She and I acted as relatives to each other. It was as if she were some stranger on the road with whom circumstances had chanced to bring me. Perhaps it was I who was an odd creature, or maybe it was my mother who was odd – I don't know. We used not to talk much. I used to have – you may be surprised – a warm feeling of being free, that there was not a human being, by father or mother, to tie me down as a tent peg to a particular spot, a particular domain. I would read and sleep, go out and come in, play outside the house, loaf around the streets, and there would be no one to order me about. Yet I had felt from childhood that I – that I was different – I mean that I was not like other children of my age: I wasn't affected by anything, I didn't cry when hit, wasn't glad if the teacher praised me in class, didn't suffer from the things the rest did. I was like something rounded, made of rubber: you throw it in the water and it doesn't get wet, you throw it on the ground and it bounces back. That was the time when we first had schools. I remember now that people were not keen about them and so the government would send its officials to scour the villages and tribal communities, while the people would hide their sons – they thought of schools as being a great evil that had come to them with the armies of occupation. I was playing with some boys outside our house when along came a man dressed in uniform riding a horse. He came to a stop above us. The other boys ran away and I stayed on, looking at the horse and the man on it. He asked me my name and I told him. "How old are you?" he said. "I don't know," I said. "Do you want to study at a school?" "What's school?" I said to him. "A nice stone building in the middle of a large garden on the banks of the Nile. The bell rings and you go into class with the other pupils – you learn reading and writing and arithmetic." "Will I wear a turban like that?" I said to the man, indicating the dome-like object on his head. The man laughed. "This isn't a turban," he said. "It's a hat." He dismounted and placed it on my head and the whole of my face disappeared inside it. "When you grow up," the man said, "and leave school and become an official in the government, you'll wear a hat like this." "I'll go to school," I said to the man. He seated me behind him on the horse and took me to just such a place as he had described, made of stone, on the banks of the Nile, surrounded by trees and flowers. We went in to see a bearded man wearing a *jibba*, who stood up, patted me on the head and said: "But where's your father?" When I told him my father was dead, he said to me: "Who's your guardian?" "I want to go to school," I said to him. The man looked at me kindly, then entered my name in a register. They asked me how old I was and I said I didn't know, and suddenly the bell rang and I fled from them and entered one of the rooms. Then the two men came along and led me off to another room, where they sat me down on a chair among other boys. At noon, when I returned to my mother, she asked me where I'd been and I told her what had happened. For a moment she glanced at me curiously, as though she wanted to hug me to her, for I saw that her face had momentarily lit up, that her eyes were bright and her lips had softened as though she wished to smile or to say something. But she did not say anything. This was a turning-point in my life. It was the first decision I had taken of my own free will.

'I don't ask you to believe what I tell you. You are entitled to wonder and to doubt – you're free. These events happened a long time ago. They are, as you'll now see, of no value. I mention them to you because they spring to mind, because certain incidents recall certain other ones.

'At any rate I devoted myself with the whole of my being to that new life. Soon I discovered in my brain a wonderful ability to learn by heart, to grasp and comprehend. On reading a book it would lodge itself solidly in my brain. No sooner had I set my mind to a problem in arithmetic than its intricacies opened up to me, melted away in my hands as though they were a piece of salt I had placed in water. I learnt to write in two weeks, after which I surged forward, nothing stopping me. My mind was like a sharp knife, cutting with cold effectiveness. I paid no attention to the astonishment of the teachers, the admiration or envy of my schoolmates. The teachers regarded me as a prodigy and the pupils began seeking my friendship, but I was busy with this wonderful machine with which I had been endowed. I was cold as a field of ice, nothing in the world could shake me.

'I covered the first stage in two years and in the intermediate school I discovered other mysteries, amongst which was the English language. My brain continued on, biting and cutting like the teeth of a plough. Words and sentences formed themselves before me as though they were mathematical equations; algebra and geometry as though they were verses of poetry. I viewed the vast world in the geography lessons as though it were a chess board. The intermediate was the furthest stage of education one could reach in those days. After three years the headmaster – who was an Englishman – said to me,

"This country hasn't got the scope for that brain of yours, so take yourself off. Go to Egypt or Lebanon or England. We have nothing further to give you." I immediately said to him: "I want to go to Cairo." He later facilitated my departure and arranged a free place for me at a secondary school in Cairo, with a scholarship from the government. This is a fact in my life: the way chance has placed in my path people who gave me a helping hand at every stage, people for whom I had no feelings of gratitude; I used to take their help as though it were some duty they were performing for me.

'When the headmaster informed me that everything had been arranged for my departure to Cairo, I went to talk to my mother. Once again she gave me that strange look. Her lips parted momentarily as though she wanted to smile, then she shut them and her face reverted to its usual state: a thick mask, or rather a series of masks. Then she disappeared for a while and brought back her purse, which she placed in my hand.

'"Had your father lived," she said to me, "he would not have chosen for you differently from what you have chosen for yourself. Do as you wish, depart or stay, it's up to you. It's your life and you're free to do with it as you will. In this purse is some money which will come in useful." That was our farewell: no tears, no kisses, no fuss. Two human beings had walked along a part of the road together, then each had gone his way. This was in fact the last thing she said to me, for I did not see her again. After long years and numerous experiences, I remembered that moment and I wept. At the time, though, I felt nothing whatsoever. I packed up my belongings in a small suitcase and took the train. No one waved to me and I spilled no tears at parting from anyone. The train journeyed off into the desert and for a while I thought of the town I had left behind me; it was like some mountain on which I had pitched my tent and in the morning I had taken up the pegs, saddled my camel and continued my travels. While we were in Wadi Halfa I thought about Cairo, my brain picturing it as another mountain, larger in size, on which I would spend a night or two, after which I would continue the journey to yet another destination.

'I remember that in the train I sat opposite a man wearing clerical garb and with a large golden cross round his neck. The man smiled at me and spoke in English, in which I answered. I remember well that amazement expressed itself on his face, his eyes opening wide directly he heard my voice. He examined my face closely, then said: "How old are you?" I told him I was fifteen, though actually I was twelve, but I was afraid he might not take me seriously. "Where are you going?" said the man. "I'm going to a secondary school in Cairo." "Alone?" he said. "Yes," I said. Again he gave me a long searching look. Before he spoke I said, "I like travelling alone. What's there to be afraid of?" At this he uttered a sentence to which at the time I did not pay much attention. Then, with a large smile lighting up his face, he said: "You speak English with astonishing fluency."

'When I arrived in Cairo I found Mr Robinson and his wife awaiting me, Mr Stockwell (the headmaster in Khartoum) having informed them I was coming. The man shook me by the hand and said, "How are you, Mr Sa'eed?" "Very well thank you, Mr Robinson," I told him. Then the man introduced me to his wife, and all of a sudden I felt the woman's arms embracing me and her lips on my cheek. At that moment, as I stood on the station platform amidst a welter of sounds and sensations, with the woman's arms round my neck, her mouth on my cheek, the smell of her body – a strange, European smell – tickling my nose, her breast touching my chest, I felt – I, a boy of twelve – a vague sexual yearning I had never previously experienced. I felt as though Cairo, that large mountain to which my camel had carried me, was a European woman just like Mrs Robinson, its arms embracing me, its perfume and the odour of its body filling my nostrils. In my mind her eyes were the colour of Cairo: grey-green, turning at night to a twinkling like that of a firefly. "Mr Sa'eed, you're a person quite devoid of a sense of fun," Mrs Robinson used to say to me and it was true that I never used to laugh. "Can't you ever forget your intellect?" she would say, laughing, and on the day they sentenced me at the Old Bailey to seven years' imprisonment, I found no bosom except hers on which to rest my head. "Don't cry, dear child," she had said to me, patting my head. They had no children. Mr Robinson knew Arabic well and was interested in Islamic thought and architecture, and it was with them that I visited Cairo's mosques, its museums and antiquities. The district of Cairo they loved best was al-Azhar. When our feet wearied of walking about we'd take ourselves off to a café close by the al-Azhar Mosque where we would drink tamarind juice and Mr Robinson would recite the poetry of al-Ma'arri. At that time I was wrapped up in myself and paid no attention to the love they showered on me. Mrs Robinson was a buxom woman and with a bronze complexion that harmonized with Cairo, as though she were a picture tastefully chosen to go with the colour of the walls in a room. I would look at the hair of her armpits and would have a sensation of panic. Perhaps she knew I desired her. But she was sweet, the sweetest woman I've known; she used to laugh gaily and was as tender to me as a mother to her own son.

'They were on the quayside when the ship set sail with me from Alexandria. I saw her far-away waving to me with her handkerchief, then drying her tears with it, her husband at her side, his hands on his hips; even at that distance I could almost see the limpid blueness of his eyes. However I was not sad. My sole concern was to reach London, another mountain, larger than Cairo, where I knew not how many nights I would stay. Though I was then fifteen, I looked nearer twenty, for I was as taut and firm-looking as an inflated waterskin. Behind me was a story of spectacular success at school, my sole weapon being that sharp knife inside my skull, while within my breast was a hard, cold feeling – as if it had been cast in rock. And when the sea swallowed up the shore and the waves heaved under the ship and the blue horizon encircled us, I immediately felt an overwhelming intimacy with the sea. I knew this green, infinite giant, as though it were roving back and forth within my ribs. The whole of the journey I savoured that feeling of being nowhere, alone, before and behind me either eternity or nothingness. The surface of the sea when calm is another mirage, ever changing and shifting, like the mask on my mother's face. Here, too, was a desert laid out in blue-green, calling me, calling me. The mysterious call led me to the coast of Dover, to London and tragedy.

'Later I followed the same road on my return, asking myself during the whole journey whether it would have been possible to have avoided any of what happened. The string of the bow is drawn taut and the arrow must needs shoot forth. I look to right and left, at the dark greenness, at the Saxon villages standing on the fringes of hills. The red roofs of houses vaulted like the backs of cows. A transparent veil of mist is spread above the valleys. What a great amount of water there is here, how vast the greenness! And all those colours! The smell of the place is strange, like that of Mrs Robinson's body. The sounds have a crisp impact on the ear, like the rustle of birds' wings. This is an ordered world; its houses, fields, and trees are ranged in accordance with a plan. The streams too do not follow a zigzag course but flow between artificial banks. The train stops at a station for a few minutes; hurriedly people get off, hurriedly others get on, then the train moves off again. No fuss.

'I thought of my life in Cairo. Nothing untoward had occurred. My knowledge had increased and several minor incidents had happened to me; a fellow student had fallen in love with me and had then hated me. "You're not a human being," she had said to me. "You're a heartless machine." I had loafed around the streets of Cairo, visited the opera, gone to the theatre, and once I had swum across the Nile. Nothing whatsoever had happened except that the waterskin had distended further, the bowstring had become more taut. The arrow will shoot forth towards other unknown horizons.

'I looked at the smoke from the engine vanishing to where it is dispersed by the wind and merges into the veil of mist spread across the valleys. Falling into a short sleep, I dreamt I was praying alone at the Citadel Mosque. It was illuminated with thousands of chandeliers, and the red marble glowed as I prayed alone. When I woke up there was the smell of incense in my nose and I found that the train was approaching London. Cairo was a city of laughter, just as Mrs Robinson was a woman of laughter. She had wanted me to call her by her first name – Elizabeth – but I always used to call her by her married name. From her I learnt to love Bach's music, Keats's poetry, and from her I heard for the first time of Mark Twain. And yet I enjoyed nothing. Mrs Robinson would laugh and say to me, "Can't you ever forget your intellect?" Would it have been possible to have avoided any of what happened? At that time I was on the way back. I remembered what the priest had said to me when I was on my way to Cairo: "All of us, my son, are in the last resort travelling alone." He was fingering the cross on his chest and his face lit up in a big smile as he added: "You speak English with astonishing fluency." The language, though, which I now heard for the first time is not like the language I had learnt at school. These are living voices and have another ring. My mind was like a keen knife. But the language is not my language; I had learnt to be eloquent in it through perseverance. And the train carried me to Victoria Station and to the world of Jean Morris.

'Everything which happened before my meeting her was a premonition; everything I did after I killed her was an apology, not for killing her, but for the lie that was my life. I was twenty-five when I met her at a party in Chelsea. The door, and a long passageway leading to the entrance hall. She opened the door and lingered; she appeared to my gaze under the faint lamplight like a mirage shimmering in a desert. I was drunk, my glass two-thirds empty. With me were two girls; I was saying lewd things to them and they were laughing. She came towards us with wide strides, placing the weight of her body on the right foot so that her buttocks inclined leftwards. She was looking at me as she approached. She stopped opposite me and gave me a look of arrogance, coldness, and something else. I opened my mouth to speak, but she had gone. "Who's that female?" I said to my two companions.

'London was emerging from the war and the oppressive atmosphere of the Victorian era. I got to know the pubs of Chelsea, the clubs of Hampstead, and the gatherings of Bloomsbury. I would read poetry, talk of religion and philosophy, discuss paintings, and say things about the spirituality of the East. I would do everything possible to entice a woman to my bed. Then I would go after some new prey. My soul contained not a drop of sense of fun – just as Mrs Robinson had said. The women I enticed to my bed included girls from the Salvation Army, Quaker societies and Fabian gatherings. When the Liberals, the Conservatives, Labour, or the Communists, held a meeting, I would saddle my camel and go. "You're ugly," Jean Morris said to me on the second occasion. "I've never seen an uglier face than yours." I opened my mouth to speak but she had gone. At that instant, drunk as I was, I swore I would one day make her pay for that. When I woke up, Ann Hammond was beside me in the bed. What was it that attracted Ann Hammond to me? Her father was an officer in the Royal Engineers, her mother from a rich family in Liverpool. She proved an easy prey. When I first met her she was less than twenty and was studying Oriental languages at Oxford. She was lively, with a gay intelligent face and eyes that sparkled with curiosity. When she saw me, she saw a dark twilight like a false dawn. Unlike me, she yearned for tropical climes, cruel suns, purple horizons. In her eyes I was a symbol of all her hankerings. I am South that yearns for the North and the ice. Ann Hammond spent her childhood at a convent school. Her aunt was the wife of a Member of Parliament. In my bed I transformed her into a harlot. My bedroom was a graveyard that looked on to a garden; its curtains were pink and had been chosen with care, the carpeting was of a warm greenness, the bed spacious, with swansdown cushions. There were small electric lights, red, blue, and violet, placed in certain corners; on the walls were large mirrors, so that when I slept with a woman it was as if I slept with a whole harem simultaneously. The room was heavy with the smell of burning sandalwood and incense, and in the bathroom were pungent Eastern perfumes, lotions, unguents, powders, and pills. My bedroom was like an operating theatre in a hospital. There is a still pool in the depths of every woman that I knew how to stir. One day they found her dead. She had gassed herself. They also found a small piece of paper with my name on it. It contained nothing but the words: "Mr Sa'eed, may God damn you." My mind was like a sharp knife. The train carried me to Victoria Station and to the world of Jean Morris.

'In the courtroom in London I sat for weeks listening to the lawyers talking about me – as though they were talking about some person who was no concern of mine. The Public Prosecutor, Sir Arthur Higgins, had a brilliant mind. I knew him well, for he had taught me Criminal Law at Oxford and I had seen him before, at this court, in this very same room, tightening his grip on the accused as they stood in the dock. Rarely did anyone escape him. I saw men weeping and fainting after he had finished his cross examination; but this time he was wrestling with a corpse.

'"Were you the cause of Ann Hammond's suicide?"

'"I don't know."

'"And Sheila Greenwood?"

'"I don't know."

'"And Isabella Seymour?"

'"I don't know."

'"Did you kill Jean Morris?"

'"Yes."

'"Did you kill her intentionally?"

'"Yes."

'It was as though his voice came to me from another world. The man continued skilfully to draw a terrible picture of a werewolf who had been the reason for two girls committing suicide, had wrecked the life of a married woman and killed his own wife – an egoist whose whole life had been directed to the quest of pleasure. Once it occurred to me in my stupor, as I sat there listening to my former teacher, Professor Maxwell Foster-Keen, trying to save me from the gallows, that I should stand up and shout at the court: "This Mustafa Sa'eed does not exist. He's an illusion, a lie. I ask of you to rule that the lie be killed." But I remained as lifeless as a heap of ashes. Professor Maxwell Foster-Keen continued to draw a distinctive picture of the mind of a genius whom circumstances had driven to killing in a moment of mad passion. He related to them how I had been appointed a lecturer in economics at London University at the age of twenty-four. He told them that Ann Hammond and Sheila Greenwood were girls who were seeking death by every means and that they would have committed suicide whether they had met Mustafa Sa'eed or not. "Mustafa Sa'eed, gentlemen of the jury, is a noble person whose mind was able to absorb Western civilization but it broke his heart. These girls were not killed by Mustafa Sa'eed but by the germ of a deadly disease that assailed them a thousand years ago." It occurred to me that I should stand up and say to them: "This is untrue, a fabrication. It was I who killed them. I am the desert of thirst. I am no Othello. I am a lie. Why don't you sentence me to be hanged and so kill the lie?" But Professor Foster-Keen turned the trial into a conflict between two worlds, a struggle of which I was one of the victims. The train carried me to Victoria Station and to the world of Jean Morris.

'I pursued her for three years. Every day the string of the bow became more taut. It was with air that my waterskins were distended; my caravans were thirsty, and the mirage shimmered before me in the wilderness of longing; the arrow's target had been fixed and it was inevitable the tragedy would take place. "You're a savage bull that does not weary of the chase," she said to me one day. "I am tired of your pursuing me and of my running before you. Marry me." So I married her. My bedroom became

33

a theatre of war; my bed a patch of hell. When I grasped her it was like grasping at clouds, like bedding a shooting-star, like mounting the back of a Prussian military march. That bitter smile was continually on her mouth. I would stay awake all night warring with bow and sword and spear and arrows, and in the morning I would see the smile unchanged and would know that once again I had lost the combat. It was as though I were a slave Shahrayar you buy in the market for a dinar encountering a Scheherazade begging amidst the rubble of a city destroyed by plague. By day I lived with the theories of Keynes and Tawney and at night I resumed the war with bow and sword and spear and arrows. I saw the troops returning, filled with terror, from the war of trenches, of lice and epidemics. I saw them sowing the seeds of the next war in the Treaty of Versailles, and I saw Lloyd George lay the foundations of a public welfare state. The city was transformed into an extraordinary woman, with her symbols and her mysterious calls, towards whom I drove my camels till their entrails ached and I myself almost died of yearning for her. My bedroom was a spring-well of sorrow, the germ of a fatal disease. The infection had stricken these women a thousand years ago, but I had stirred up the latent depths of the disease until it had got out of control and had killed. The theatres of Leicester Square echoed with songs of love and gaiety, but my heart did not beat in time with them. Who would have thought that Sheila Greenwood would have the courage to commit suicide? A waitress in a Soho restaurant, a simple girl with a sweet smile and a sweet way of speaking.

Her people were village folk from the suburbs of Hull. I seduced her with gifts and honeyed words, and an unfaltering way of seeing things as they really are. It was my world, so novel to her, that attracted her. The smell of burning sandalwood and incense made her dizzy; she stood for a long time laughing at her image in the mirror as she fondled the ivory necklace I had placed like a noose round her beautiful neck. She entered my bedroom a chaste virgin and when she left it she was carrying the germs of self-destruction within her. She died without a single word passing her lips – my storehouse of hackneyed phrases is inexhaustible. For every occasion I possess the appropriate garb.

'"Is it not true, by way of example, that in the period between October 1922 and February 1923, that in this period alone you were living with five women simultaneously?"

'"Yes.'

'"And that you gave each one the impression you'd marry her?"

'"Yes."

'"And that you adopted a different name with each one?"

'"Yes."

'"That you were Hassan and Charles and Amin and Mustafa and Richard?"

'"Yes."

'"And yet you were writing and lecturing on a system of economics based on love not figures? Isn't it true you made your name by your appeal for humanity in economics?"

'"Yes."'

35

'Thirty years. The willow trees turned from white to green to yellow in the parks; the cuckoo sang to the spring each year. For thirty years the Albert Hall was crammed each night with lovers of Beethoven and Bach, and the presses brought out thousands of books on art and thought. The plays of Bernard Shaw were put on at The Royal Court and The Haymarket. Edith Sitwell was giving wings to poetry and The Prince of Wales's Theatre pulsated with youth and bright lights. The sea continued to ebb and flow at Bournemouth and Brighton, and the Lake District flowered year after year. The island was like a sweet tune, happy and sad, changing like a mirage with the changing of the seasons. For thirty years I was a part of all this, living in it but insensitive to its real beauty, unconcerned with everything about it except the filling of my bed each night.

'Yes. It was summer – they said that they had not known a summer like it for a hundred years. I left my house on a Saturday, sniffing the air, feeling I was about to start upon a great hunt. I reached Speakers' Corner in Hyde Park. It was packed with people. I stood listening from afar to a speaker from the West Indies talking about the colour problem. Suddenly my eyes came to rest on a woman who was craning her neck to catch a glimpse of the speaker so that her dress was lifted above her knees exposing two shapely, bronzed legs. Yes, this was my prey. I

36

walked up to her, like a boat heading towards the rapids. I stood beside her and pressed up close against her till I felt her warmth pervading me. I breathed in the odour of her body, that odour with which Mrs Robinson had met me on the platform of Cairo's railway station. I was so close to her that, becoming aware of me, she turned to me suddenly. I smiled into her face – a smile the outcome of which I knew not, except that I was determined that it should not go to waste. I also laughed lest the surprise in her face should turn to animosity. Then she smiled. I stood beside her for about a quarter of an hour, laughing when the speaker's words made her laugh – loudly so that she might be affected by the contagion of it. Then came the moment when I felt that she and I had become like a mare and foal running in harmony side by side. A sound, as though it were not my voice, issued from my throat: "What about a drink, away from this crowd and heat?" She turned her head in astonishment. This time I smiled – a broad innocent smile so that I might change astonishment into, at least, curiosity. Meanwhile I closely examined her face: each one of her features increased my conviction that this was my prey. With the instinct of a gambler I knew that this was a decisive moment. At this moment everything was possible. My smile changed to a gladness I could scarcely keep in rein as she said: "Yes, why not?" We walked along together; she beside me, a glittering figure of bronze under the July sun, a city of secrets and rapture. I was pleased she laughed so freely. Such a woman – there are many of her type in Europe – knows no fear; they accept life with gaiety and curiosity. And I am a thirsty desert, a wilderness of southern desires. As we drank tea, she asked me about my home. I related to her fabricated stories about deserts of golden sands and jungles where non-existent animals called out to one another. I told her that the streets of my country teemed with elephants and lions and that during siesta time crocodiles crawled through it. Half-credulous, half-disbelieving, she listened to me, laughing and closing her eyes, her cheeks reddening. Sometimes she would hear me out in silence, a Christian sympathy in her eyes. There came a moment when I felt I had been transformed in her eyes into a naked, primitive creature, a spear in one hand and arrows in the other, hunting elephants and lions in the jungles. This was fine. Curiosity had changed to gaiety, and gaiety to sympathy, and when I stir the still pool in its depths the sympathy will be transformed into a desire upon whose taut strings I shall play as I wish. "What race are you?" she asked me. "Are you African or Asian?"

'"I'm like Othello – Arab–African," I said to her.

'"Yes," she said, looking into my face. "Your nose is like the noses of Arabs in pictures, but your hair isn't soft and jet black like that of Arabs."

'"Yes, that's me. My face is Arab like the desert of the Empty Quarter, while my head is African and teems with a mischievous childishness."

'"You put things in such a funny way," she said laughing.

'The conversation led us to my family, and I told her – without lying this time – that I had grown up without a father. Then, returning to my lies, I gave her such terrifying descriptions of how I had lost my parents that I saw the tears well up in her eyes. I told her I was six years old at the time when my parents were drowned with thirty other people in a boat taking them from one bank of the Nile to the other. Here something occurred which was better than expressions of pity; pity in such instances is an emotion with uncertain consequences. Her eyes brightened and she cried out ecstatically:

'"The Nile."

'"Yes, the Nile."

'"Then you live on the banks of the Nile?"

'"Yes. Our house is right on the bank of the Nile, so that when I'm lying on my bed at night I put my hand out of the window and idly play with the Nile waters till sleep overtakes me."

'Mr Mustafa, the bird has fallen into the snare. The Nile, that snake god, has gained a new victim. The city has changed into a woman. It would be but a day or a week before I would pitch tent, driving my tent peg into the mountain summit. You, my lady, may not know, but you – like Carnarvon when he entered Tutankhamen's tomb – have been infected with a deadly disease which has come from you know not where and which will bring about your destruction, be it sooner or later. My store of hackneyed phrases is inexhaustible. I felt the flow of conversation firmly in my hands, like the reins of an obedient mare: I pull at them and she stops, I shake them and she advances; I move them and she moves subject to my will, to left or to right.

'"Two hours have passed without my being aware of them," I said to her. "I've not felt such happiness for a long time. And there's so much left for me to say to you and you to me. What would you say to having dinner together and continuing the conversation?"

'For a while she remained silent. I was not alarmed for I felt that satanic warmth under my diaphragm, and when I feel it I know that I am in full command of the situation. No, she would not say no. "This is an extraordinary meeting," she said. "A man I don't know invites me out. It's not right, but –" She was silent. "Yes, why not?" she then said. "There's nothing to tell from your face you're a cannibal."

'"You'll find I'm an aged crocodile who's lost its teeth," I said to her, a wave of joy stirring in the roots of my heart. "I wouldn't have the strength to eat you even if I wanted to." I reckoned I was at least fifteen years her junior, for she was a woman in the region of forty, whose body – whatever the experiences she had undergone – time had treated kindly. The fine wrinkles on her forehead and at the corners of her mouth told one not that she had grown old, but that she had ripened.

'Only then did I ask her name.

'"Isabella Seymour," she said.

'I repeated it twice, rolling it round my tongue as though eating a pear.

'"And what's *your* name?"

'"I'm – Amin. Amin Hassan."

'"I shall call you Hassan."

'With the grills and wine her features relaxed and there gushed forth – upon me – a love she felt for the whole world. I wasn't so much concerned with her love for the world, or for the cloud of sadness that crossed her face from time to time, as I was with the

40

redness of her tongue when she laughed, the fullness of her lips and the secrets lurking in the abyss of her mouth. I pictured her obscenely naked as she said: "Life is full of pain, yet we must be optimistic and face life with courage."

'Yes, I now know that in the rough wisdom that issues from the mouths of simple people lies our whole hope of salvation. A tree grows simply and your grandfather has lived and will die simply. That is the secret. You are right, my lady: courage and optimism. But until the meek inherit the earth, until the armies are disbanded, the lamb grazes in peace beside the wolf and the child plays water-polo in the river with the crocodile, until that time of happiness and love comes along, I for one shall continue to express myself in this twisted manner. And when, puffing, I reach the mountain peak and implant the banner, collect my breath and rest – that, my lady, is an ecstasy greater to me than love, than happiness. Thus I mean you no harm, except to the extent that the sea is harmful when ships are wrecked against its rocks, and to the extent that the lightning is harmful when it rends a tree in two. This last idea converged in my mind on the tiny hairs on her right arm near to the wrist, and I noticed that the hair on her arms was thicker than with most women, and this led my thoughts to other hair. It would certainly be as soft and abundant as cypress-grass on the banks of a stream. As though the thought had radiated from my mind to hers she sat up straight. "Why do you look so sad?" she said.

'"Do I look sad? On the contrary, I'm very happy."

'The tender look came back into her eyes as she

stretched out her hand and took hold of mine. "Do you know that my mother's Spanish?" she said.

'"That, then, explains everything. It explains our meeting by chance, our spontaneous mutual understanding as though we had got to know each other centuries ago. Doubtless one of my forefathers was a soldier in Tarik ibn Ziyad's army. Doubtless he met one of your ancestors as she gathered in the grapes from an orchard in Seville. Doubtless he fell in love with her at first sight and she with him. He lived with her for a time, then left her and went off to Africa. There he married again and I was one of his progeny in Africa, and you have come from his progeny in Spain."

'These words, also the low lights and the wine, made her happy. She gave out throaty, gurgling laughs.

'"What a devil you are!" she said.

'For a moment I imagined to myself the Arab soldiers' first meeting with Spain: like me at this instant sitting opposite Isabella Seymour, a southern thirst being dissipated in the mountain passes of history in the north. However, I seek not glory, for the likes of me do not seek glory.

'After a month of feverish desire I turned the key in the door with her at my side, a fertile Andalusia; after that I led her across the short passageway to the bedroom where the smell of burning sandalwood and incense assailed her, filling her lungs with a perfume she little knew was deadly. In those days, when the summit lay a mere arm's length away from me, I would be enveloped in a tragic calm. All the fever and throbbing of the heart, the strain of nerves,

42

would be transformed into the calm of a surgeon as he opens up the patient's stomach. I knew that the short road along which we walked together to the bedroom was, for her, a road of light redolent with the aroma of magnanimity and devotion, but which to me was the last step before attaining the peak of selfishness. I waited by the edge of the bed, as though condensing that moment in my mind, and cast a cold eye at the pink curtains and large mirrors, the lights lurking in the corners of the room, then at the shapely bronze statue before me. When we were at the climax of the tragedy she cried out weakly, "No. No." This will be of no help to you now. The critical moment when it was in your power to refrain from taking the first step has been lost. I caught you unawares; at that time it was in your power to say "No". As for now the flood of events has swept you along, as it does every person, and you are no longer capable of doing anything. Were every person to know when to refrain from taking the first step many things would have been changed. Is the sun wicked when it turns the hearts of millions of human beings into sand-strewn deserts in which the throat of the nightingale is parched with thirst? Lingeringly I passed the palm of my hand over her neck and kissed her in the fountain-heads of her sensitivity. With every touch, with every kiss, I felt a muscle in her body relax; her face glowed and her eyes sparkled with a sudden brightness. She gazed hard and long at me as though seeing me as a symbol rather than reality. I heard her saying to me in an imploring voice of surrender "I love you," and there answered her voice a weak cry from

43

the depths of my consciousness calling on me to desist. But the summit was only a step away, after which I would recover my breath and rest. At the climax of our pain there passed through my head clouds of old, far-off memories, like a vapour rising up from a salt lake in the middle of the desert. She burst into agonized, consuming tears, while I gave myself up to a feverishly tense sleep.'

It was a steamingly hot July night, the
Nile that year having experienced one of those
floodings that occur once every twenty or thirty
years and become legendary – something for fathers
to talk to their sons about. Water covered most of
the land lying between the river bank and the edge of
the desert where the houses stood, and the fields
became like islands amidst the water. The men
moved between the houses and the fields in small
boats or covered the distance swimming. Mustafa
Sa'eed was, as far as I knew, an excellent swimmer.
My father told me – for I was in Khartoum at the
time – that they heard women screaming in the
quarter after the evening prayers and, on hurrying to
the source of the sound, had found that the screaming was coming from Mustafa Sa'eed's house.
Though he was in the habit of returning from the
fields at sunset, his wife had waited for him in vain.
On asking about him here and there she was told he
had been seen in his field, though some thought he
had returned home with the rest of the men. The
whole village, carrying lamps, combed the river
bank, while some put out in boats, but though they
searched the whole night through it was without
avail. Telephone messages were sent to the police
stations right along the Nile as far as Karma, but
Mustafa Sa'eed's body was not among those washed

45

Mustafa's death ?

up on the river bank that week. In the end they pre-
sumed he must have been drowned and that his body
had come to rest in the bellies of the crocodiles
infesting the waters.

As for me, I am sometimes seized by the feeling
which came over me that night when, suddenly and
without my being at all prepared for it, I had heard
him quoting English poetry, a drink in his hand,
his body buried deep in his chair, his legs out-
stretched, the light reflected on his face, his eyes, it
seemed to me, abstractedly wandering towards the
horizon deep within himself, and with darkness all
around us outside as though satanic forces were
combining to strangle the lamplight. Occasionally
the disturbing thought occurs to me that Mustafa
Sa'eed never happened, that he was in fact a lie, a
phantom, a dream or a nightmare that had come to
the people of that village one suffocatingly dark
night, and when they opened their eyes to the sun-
light he was nowhere to be seen.

Only the lesser part of the night still remained when
I had left Mustafa Sa'eed's house. I left with a feeling
of tiredness – perhaps due to having sat for so long.
Yet having no desire to sleep, I wandered off into
the narrow winding lanes of the village, my face
touched by the cold night breezes that blow in
heavy with dew from the north, heavy too with the
scent of acacia blossom and animal dung, the scent of

46

earth that has just been irrigated after the thirst of days, and the scent of half-ripe corn cobs and the aroma of lemon trees. The village was as usual silent at that hour of the night except for the puttering of the water pump on the bank, the occasional barking of a dog, and the crowing of a lone cock who prematurely sensed the arrival of the dawn and the answering crow of another. Then silence reigned. Passing by Wad Rayyes's low-lying house at the bend in the lane, I saw a dim light coming from the small window, and heard his wife give a cry of pleasure. I felt ashamed at having been privy to something I shouldn't have been: it wasn't right of me to stay awake wandering round the streets while everyone else was asleep in bed. I know this village street by street, house by house; I know too the ten domed shrines that stand in the middle of the cemetery on the edge of the desert high at the top of the village; the graves too I know one by one, having visited them with my father and mother and with my grandfather. I know those who inhabit these graves, both those who died before my father was born and those who have died since my birth. I have walked in more than a hundred funeral processions, have helped with the digging of the grave and have stood alongside it in the crush of people as the dead man was cushioned around with stones and the earth heaped in over him. I have done this in the early mornings, in the intensity of the noonday heat in the summer months, and at night with lamps in our hands. I have known the fields too ever since the days when there were water-wheels, and the times of drought when the men forsook the fields and when

47

the fertile land stretching from the edge of the desert, where the houses stood, to the bank of the Nile was turned into a barren windswept wilderness. Then came the water pumps, followed by the co-operative societies, and those men who had migrated came back; the land returned to its former state, producing maize in summer and wheat in winter. All this I had been a witness to ever since I opened my eyes on life, yet I had never seen the village at such a late hour of the night. No doubt that large, brilliantly blue star was the Morning Star. At such an hour, just before dawn, the sky seemed nearer to the earth, and the village was enveloped in a hazy light that gave it the look of being suspended between earth and sky. As I crossed the patch of sand that separates the house of Wad Rayyes from that of my grandfather, I remembered the picture that Mustafa Sa'eed had depicted, remembered it with the same feeling of embarrassment as came to me when I overheard the love play of Wad Rayyes with his wife: two thighs, opened wide and white. I reached the door of my grandfather's house and heard him reading his collects in preparation for the morning prayers. Doesn't he ever sleep? My grandfather's voice praying was the last sound I heard before I went to sleep and the first I heard on waking. He had been like this for I don't know how many years, as though he were something immutable in a dynamic world. Suddenly I felt my spirits being reinvigorated as sometimes happens after a long period of depression: my brain cleared and the black thoughts stirred up by the story of Mustafa Sa'eed were dispersed. Now the village was not suspended between sky and earth but was stable: the houses were houses, the trees trees, and the sky was clear and faraway. Was it likely that what had happened to Mustafa Sa'eed could have happened to me? He had said that he was a lie, so was I also a lie? I am from here – is not this reality enough? I too had lived with them. But I had lived with them superficially, neither loving nor hating them. I used to treasure within me the image of this little village, seeing it wherever I went with the eye of my imagination.

Sometimes during the summer months in London, after a downpour of rain, I would breathe in the smell of it, and at odd fleeting moments before sunset I would see it. At the latter end of the night the foreign voices would reach my ears as though they were those of my people out here. I must be one of those birds that exist only in one region of the world. True I studied poetry, but that means nothing. I could equally well have studied engineering, agriculture, or medicine; they are all means to earning a living. I would imagine the faces over there as being brown or black so that they would look like the faces of people I knew. Over there is like here, neither better nor worse. But I am from here, just as the date palm standing in the courtyard of our house has grown in *our* house and not in anyone else's. The fact that they came to our land, I know not why, does that mean that we should poison our present and our future? Sooner or later they will leave our country, just as many people throughout history left many countries. The railways, ships, hospitals, factories and schools will be ours and we'll speak their language without either a sense of guilt or a sense of

colonialism

brilliant, like Sayeed

49

gratitude. Once again we shall be as we were – ordinary people – and if we are lies we shall be lies of our own making.

Such thoughts accompanied me to my bed and thereafter to Khartoum, where I took up my work in the Department of Education. Mustafa Sa'eed died two years ago, but I still continue to meet up with him from time to time. I lived for twenty-five years without having heard of him or seen him; then, all of a sudden, I find him in a place where the likes of him are not usually encountered. Thus Mustafa Sa'eed has, against my will, become a part of my world, a thought in my brain, a phantom that does not want to take itself off. And thus too I experience a remote feeling of fear, fear that it is just conceivable that simplicity is not everything. Mustafa Sa'eed said that my grandfather knows the secret. 'A tree grows simply and your grandfather has lived and will die simply.' Just like that. But suppose he was making fun of my simplicity? On a train journey between Khartoum and El-Obeid I travelled in the same compartment with a retired civil servant. When the train moved out of Kosti the conversation had brought us up to his school days. I learnt from him that a number of my chiefs at the Ministry of Education were contemporaries of his at school, some having been in the same form with him. The man mentioned that so-and-so at the Ministry of Agriculture was a schoolmate of his, that such-and-such an engineer was in the form above him, that so-and-so, the merchant who'd grown rich during the war years, had been the stupidest creature in the form, and that the famous surgeon so-and-so was the best right-wing in the whole school at that time. Suddenly I saw the man's face light up, his eyes sparkle, as he said in an excited, animated voice: 'How strange! Can you imagine? I quite forgot the most brilliant student in our form and before now he's never come to my mind since he left school. Only now do I remember him. Yes – Mustafa Sa'eed.'

Once again there was that feeling that the ordinary things before one's very eyes were becoming un-ordinary. I saw the carriage window and the door emerge and it seemed to me that the light reflected from the man's glasses – in an instant that was no longer than the twinkling of an eye – gave off a dazzling flash, bright as the sun at its height. Certainly the world at that moment appeared different also in relation to the retired Mamur in that a complete experience, outside his consciousness, had suddenly come within his reach. When I first saw his face I reckoned him to be in his middle sixties. Looking at him now as he continued to recount his faraway memories, I see a man who is not a day over forty.

'Yes, Mustafa Sa'eed was the most brilliant student of our day. We were in the same form together and he used to sit directly in front of our row, on the left. How strange! How had he not come to my mind before, seeing that at that time he was a real prodigy? He was the most well-known student at Gordon College, better known than the members of the first eleven, the prefects of the boarding houses, those who spoke at literary evenings, those who wrote in the wall newspapers, and the leading actors in the dramatic groups. He took part in none of these sorts of activities. Isolated and arrogant, he spent his time alone, either reading or going for long walks. We were all boarders in those days at Gordon College, even those of us who were from the three towns of Khartoum, Khartoum North and Omdurman. He was brilliant at everything, nothing being too difficult for his amazing brain. The tone in which the masters addressed him was different from that in which they talked to us, especially the English language teachers; it was as though they were giving the lesson to him alone and excluding the rest of the students.'

The man was silent for a while and I had a strong desire to tell him that I knew Mustafa Sa'eed, that circumstances had thrown him in my path and that he had recounted his life story to me one dark and torrid night; that he had spent his last days in an obscure village at the bend of the Nile, that he had been drowned, had perhaps committed suicide, and that he had made me of all people guardian of his two sons. I said nothing, however, and it was the retired Mamur who continued:

'Mustafa Sa'eed covered his period of education in the Sudan at one bound – as if he were having a race with time. While we remained on at Gordon College, he was sent on a scholarship to Cairo and later to London. He was the first Sudanese to be sent on a scholarship abroad. He was the spoilt child of the English and we all envied him and expected he would achieve great things. We used to articulate English words as though they were Arabic and were unable to pronounce two consonants together without putting a vowel in between, whereas Mustafa Sa'eed would contort his mouth and thrust out his lips and the words would issue forth as though from the mouth of one whose mother tongue it was. This would fill us with annoyance and admiration at one and the same time. With a combination of admiration and spite we nicknamed him "the black Englishman". In our day the English language was the key to the future: no one had a chance without it. Gordon College was actually little more than an intermediate school where they used to give us just enough education for filling junior government posts. When I left, I worked first as a cashier in the district of Fasher and after strenuous efforts they allowed me to sit for the Administration Examination. Thirty years I spent as a sub-Mamur – imagine it. Just a mere two years before retirement I was promoted to Mamur. The English District Commissioner was a god who had a free hand over an area larger than the whole of the British Isles and lived in an enormous palace full of servants and guarded by troops. They used to behave like gods. They would employ us, the junior government officials who were natives of the country, to bring in the taxes. The people would grumble and complain to the English Commissioner, and naturally it was the English Commissioner who was indulgent and showed mercy. And in this way they sowed hatred in the hearts of the people for us, their kinsmen, and love for the colonizers, the intruders. Mark these words of mine, my son. Has not the country become independent? Have we not become free men in our own country? Be sure, though, that they will direct our affairs from afar. This is because they have left behind them people who think as they do. They showed favour to nonentities – and it was

postcolonial / neo colonial neo historicism

such people that occupied the highest positions in the days of the English. We were certain that Mustafa Sa'eed would make his mark. His father was from the Ababda, the tribe living between Egypt and the Sudan. It was they who helped Slatin Pasha escape when he was the prisoner of the Khalifa El-Ta'aishi, after which they worked as guides for Kitchener's army when he reconquered the Sudan. It is said that his mother was a slave from the south, from the tribes of Zandi or Baria – God knows. It was the nobodies who had the best jobs in the days of the English.'

The retired Mamur was snoring away fast asleep when the train passed by the Sennar Dam, which the English had built in 1925, heading westwards to El-Obeid, on the single track stretching out across the desert like a rope bridge between two savage mountains, with a vast bottomless abyss between them. Poor Mustafa Sa'eed. He was supposed to make his mark in the world of Commissioners and Mamurs, yet he hadn't even found himself a grave to rest his body in, in this land that stretches across a million square miles. I remember his saying that before passing sentence on him at the Old Bailey the judge had said, 'Mr Sa'eed, despite your academic prowess you are a stupid man. In your spiritual make-up there is a dark spot, and thus it was that you squandered the noblest gift that God has bestowed upon people – the gift of love.' I remembered too that when I emerged from Mustafa Sa'eed's house that night the waning moon had risen to the height of a man on the eastern horizon and that I had said to myself that the moon had had her talons clipped. I don't know

Said stupid?
squandered love.

why it looked to me as if the moon's talons had been clipped.

Sudanese lecturer (ex-London)

?

Englishman from Min. of Finance

In Khartoum too the phantom of Mustafa Sa'eed appeared to me less than a month after my conversation with the retired Mamur, like a genie who has been released from his prison and will continue thereafter to whisper in men's ears. To say what? I don't know. We were in the house of a young Sudanese who was lecturing at the University and had been studying in England at the same time as I, and among those present was an Englishman who worked in the Ministry of Finance. We got on to the subject of mixed marriages and the conversation changed from being general to discussing particular instances. Who were those who had married European women? Who had married English women? Who was the first Sudanese to marry an English woman? So-and-so? No. So-and-so? No. Suddenly – Mustafa Sa'eed. The person who mentioned his name was the young lecturer at the University and on his face was that very same expression of joy I had glimpsed on the retired Mamur's face. Under Khartoum's star-studded sky in early winter the young man went on to say, 'Mustafa Sa'eed was the first Sudanese to marry an Englishwoman, in fact he was the first to marry a European of any kind. I don't think you will have heard of him, for he took himself off abroad long ago. He married in England and took

55

British nationality. Funny that no one remembers him, in spite of the fact that he played such an important role in the plottings of the English in the Sudan during the late thirties. He was one of their most faithful supporters. The Foreign Office employed him on dubious missions to the Middle East and he was one of the secretaries of the conference held in London in 1936. He's now a millionaire living like a lord in the English countryside.'

Without realizing it I found myself saying out loud, 'On his death Mustafa Sa'eed left six acres, three cows, an ox, two donkeys, ten goats, five sheep, thirty date palms, twenty-three acacia, sayal and harraz trees, twenty-five lemon, and a like number of orange, trees, nine ardebs of wheat and nine of maize, and a house made up of five rooms and a diwan, also a further room of red brick, rectangular in shape, with green windows, and a roof that was not flat as those of the rest of the rooms but triangular like the back of an ox, and nine hundred and thirty-seven pounds, three piastres and five milliemes in cash.'

In the instant it takes for a flash of lightning to come and go I saw in the eyes of the young man sitting opposite me a patently live and tangible feeling of terror. I saw it in the fixed look of his eyes, the tremor of the eyelid, and the slackening of the lower jaw. If he had not been frightened, why should he have asked me this question: 'Are you his son?'

He asked me this question though he too was unaware of why he had uttered these words, knowing as he does full well who I am. Though not fellow students, we had none the less been in England at the same time and had met up on a number of occasions, more than once drinking beer together in the pubs of Knightsbridge. So, in an instant outside the boundaries of time and place, things appear to him too as unreal. Everything seems probable. He too could be Mustafa Sa'eed's son, his brother, or his cousin. The world in that instant, as brief as the blinking of an eyelid, is made up of countless probabilities, as though Adam and Eve had just fallen from Paradise.

All these probabilities settled down into a single state of actuality when I laughed, and the world reverted to what it had been – persons with known faces and known names and known jobs, under the star-studded sky of Khartoum in early winter. He too laughed and said, 'How crazy of me! Of course you're not Mustafa Sa'eed's son or even a relative of his – perhaps you'd never even heard of him in your life before. I forgot that you poets have your flights of fancy.'

Somewhat bitterly I thought that, whether I liked it or not, I was assumed by people to be a poet because I had spent three years delving into the life of an obscure English poet and had returned to teach pre-Islamic literature in secondary schools before being promoted to an Inspector of Primary Education.

Here the Englishman intervened to say that he didn't know the truth of what was said concerning the role Mustafa Sa'eed had played in the English political plottings in the Sudan; what he did know was that Mustafa Sa'eed was not a reliable economist. 'I read some of the things he wrote about what he called "the economics of colonization". The over-riding characteristic of his writings was that his statistics were not to be trusted. He belonged to the Fabian school of economists who hid behind a screen of generalities so as to escape facing up to facts supported by figures. Justice, Equality, and Socialism – mere words. The economist isn't a writer like Charles Dickens or a political reformer like Roosevelt – he's an instrument, a machine that has no value without facts, figures, and statistics; the most he can do is to define the relationship between one fact and another, between one figure and another. As for making figures say one thing rather than another, that is the concern of rulers and politicians. The world is in no need of more politicians. No, this Mustafa Sa'eed of yours was not an economist to be trusted.'

I asked him if he had ever met Mustafa Sa'eed.

'No, I never did. He left Oxford a good while before me, but I heard bits and pieces about him from here and there. It seems he was a great one for the women. He built quite a legend of a sort round himself – the handsome black man courted in Bohemian circles. It seems he was a show-piece exhibited by members of the aristocracy who in the twenties and early thirties were affecting liberalism. It is said he was a friend of Lord-this and Lord-that. He was also one of the darlings of the English left. That was bad luck for him, because it is said he was intelligent. There's nothing in the whole world worse than leftist economists. Even his academic post – I don't know exactly what it was – I had the impression he got for reasons of this kind. It was as though they wanted to say: Look how tolerant and liberal we are! This African is just like one of us! He has married a daughter of ours and works with us on an equal footing! If you only knew, this sort of European is no less evil than the madmen who believe in the supremacy of the white man in South Africa and in the southern states of America. The same exaggerated emotional energy bears either to the extreme right or to the extreme left. If only he had stuck to academic studies he'd have found real friends of all nationalities, and you'd have heard of him here. He would certainly have returned and benefited with his knowledge this country in which superstitions hold sway. And here you are now believing in superstitions of a new sort: the superstition of industrialization, the superstition of nationalization, the superstition of Arab unity, the superstition of African unity. Like children you believe that in the bowels of the earth lies a treasure you'll attain by some miracle, and that you'll solve all your difficulties and set up a Garden of Paradise. Fantasies. Waking dreams. Through facts, figures, and statistics you can accept your reality, live together with it, and attempt to bring about changes within the limits of your potentialities. It was within the capacity of a man like Mustafa Sa'eed to play a not inconsiderable role in furthering this if he had not been transformed into a buffoon at the hands of a small group of idiotic Englishmen.'

While Mansour set out to refute Richard's views, I gave myself up to my thoughts. What was the use of arguing? This man – Richard – was also fanatical. Everyone's fanatical in one way or another. Perhaps

fanaticism

we do believe in the superstitions he mentioned, yet he believes in a new, a contemporary superstition – the superstition of statistics. So long as we believe in a god, let it be a god that is omnipotent. But of what use are statistics? The white man, merely because he has ruled us for a period of our history, will for a long time continue to have for us that feeling of contempt the strong have for the weak. Mustafa Sa'eed said to them, 'I have come to you as a conqueror.' A melodramatic phrase certainly. But their own coming too was not a tragedy as we imagine, nor yet a blessing as they imagine. It was a melodramatic act which with the passage of time will change into a mighty myth. I heard Mansour say to Richard, 'You transmitted to us the disease of your capitalist economy. What did you give us except for a handful of capitalist companies that drew off our blood – and still do?' Richard said to him, 'All this shows that you cannot manage to live without us. You used to complain about colonialism and when we left you created the legend of neo-colonialism. It seems that our presence, in an open or undercover form, is as indispensable to you as air and water.' They were not angry: they said such things to each other as they laughed, a stone's throw from the Equator, with a bottomless historical chasm separating the two of them.

But I would hope you will not entertain
the idea, dear sirs, that Mustafa Sa'eed had become
an obsession that was ever with me in my comings
and goings. Sometimes months would pass without
his crossing my mind. In any case, he had died, by
drowning or by suicide – God alone knows. Thousands of people die every day. Were we to pause and
consider why each one of them died, and how –
what would happen to us, the living? The world
goes on whether we choose for it to do so or in
defiance of us. And I, like millions of mankind, walk
and move, generally by force of habit, in a long
caravan that ascends and descends, encamps, and
then proceeds on its way. Life in this caravan is not
altogether bad. You no doubt are aware of this.
The going may be hard by day, the wilderness
sweeping out before us like shoreless seas; we pour
with sweat, our throats are parched with thirst, and
we reach the frontier beyond which we think we
cannot go. Then the sun sets, the air grows cool,
and millions of stars twinkle in the sky. We eat and
drink and the singer of the caravan breaks into song.
Some of us pray in a group behind the Sheikh,
others form ourselves into circles to dance and sing
and clap. Above us the sky is warm and compassionate. Sometimes we travel by night for as long as
we have a mind to, and when the white thread is

distinguished from the black we say, 'When dawn breaks the travellers are thankful that they have journeyed by night.' If occasionally we are deceived by a mirage, and if our heads, feverish from the action of heat and thirst, sometimes bubble with ideas devoid of any basis of validity, no harm is done. The spectres of night dissolve with the dawn, the fever of day is cooled by the night breeze. Is there any alternative?

Thus I used to spend two months a year in that small village at the bend of the Nile where the river, after flowing from south to north, suddenly turns almost at right angles and flows from west to east. It is wide and deep here and in the middle of the water are little islands of green over which hover white birds. On both banks are thick plantations of date palms, with water-wheels turning, and from time to time a water pump. The men are bare-chested; wearing long under-trousers, they cut or sow, and when the steamer passes by them like a castle floating in the middle of the Nile, they stand up straight and turn to it for a while and then go back to what they were doing. It passes this place at midday once a week, and there is still the vestige of the reflected shadows of the date palms on the water disturbed by the waves set in motion by the steamer's engines. A raucous whistle blares out, which will no doubt be heard by my people as they sit drinking their midday coffee at home. From afar the stopping-place comes into view: a white platform with a line of sycamore trees. On both banks there is activity: people on donkeys and others on foot, while out from the bank opposite the landing stage little boats and sailing ships set forth. The steamer turns round itself so the engines won't be working against the current. A fairly large gathering of men and women is there to meet it. That is my father, those my uncles and my cousins; they have tied their donkeys to the sycamore trees. No fog separates them from me this time, for I am coming from Khartoum only, after an absence of no more than seven months. I see them with a matter-of-fact eye: their galabias clean but unironed, their turbans whiter than their galabias, their moustaches ranging between long and short, between black and white; some of them have beards, and those who have not grown beards are unshaven. Among their donkeys is a tall black one I have not seen before. They regard the steamer without interest as it casts anchor and the people crowd round where the passengers disembark. They are waiting for me outside and do not hasten forward to meet me. They shake hands hurriedly with me and my wife but smother the child with kisses, taking it in turns to carry her, while the donkeys bear us off to the village. This is how it has been with me ever since I was a student at school, uninterrupted except for that long stay abroad I have already told you about. On the way to the village I ask them about the black donkey and my father says, 'A bedouin fellow cheated your uncle. He took from him the white donkey you know and five pounds as well.' I didn't know which of my uncles had been cheated by the bedouin till I heard the voice of my uncle Abdul Karim say, 'I swear I'll divorce if she isn't the most beautiful donkey in the whole place. She's more a thoroughbred mare than a donkey. If I wanted I could find somebody who'd pay me thirty pounds for her.' My uncle Abdurrahman laughs and says, 'If she's a mare, she's a barren one. There's no use at all in a donkey that doesn't foal.' I then asked about this year's date crop, though I knew the answer in advance. 'No use at all.' They say it in one voice and every year the answer's the same, and I realize that the situation isn't as they say. We pass by a red brick building on the Nile bank, half finished, and when I ask them about it my uncle Abdul Mannan says, 'A hospital. They've been at it for a whole year and can't finish it. It's a hopeless government.' I tell him that when I was here only seven months ago they hadn't even started building it, but this has no effect on my uncle Abdul Mannan, who says, 'All they're any good at is coming to us every two or three years with their hordes of people, their lorries and their posters: Long live so-and-so, down with so-and-so. We were spared all this hullabaloo in the days of the English.' In fact a group of people in an old lorry passes us shouting, 'Long live the National Democratic Socialist Party.' Are these the people who are called *peasants* in books? Had I told my grandfather that revolutions are made in his name, that governments are set up and brought down for his sake, he would have laughed. The idea appears actually incongruous, in the same way as the life and death of Mustafa Sa'eed in such a place seems incredible. Mustafa Sa'eed used regularly to attend prayers in the mosque. Why did he exaggerate in the way he acted out that comic role? Had he come to this faraway village seeking peace of mind? Perhaps the answer lay in that rectangular room with the green

64

windows. What do I expect? Do I expect to find him seated on a chair alone in the darkness? Or do I expect to find him strung up by the neck on a rope dangling from the ceiling? And the letter he has left me in an envelope sealed with red wax, when had he written it?

'I leave my wife, two sons, and all my worldly goods in your care, knowing that you will act honourably in every respect. My wife knows about all my property and is free to do with it as she pleases. I have confidence in her judgment. However, I would ask you to do this service for a man who did not have the good fortune to get to know you as he would have liked: to give my family your kind attention, and to be a help, a counsellor and an adviser to my two sons and to do your best to spare them the pangs of wanderlust. Spare them the pangs of wanderlust and help them to have a normal upbringing and to take up worthwhile work. I leave you the key of my private room where you will perhaps find what you are looking for. I know you to be suffering from undue curiosity where I am concerned – something for which I can find no justification. Whatever my life has been it contains no warning or lesson for anyone. Were it not for my realization that knowledge of my past by the village would have hindered my leading the life I had chosen for myself in their midst there would have been no justification for secrecy. You are released from the pledge you took upon yourself that night and can talk as you please. If you are unable to resist the curiosity in yourself, then you will find, in that room that has never before been entered by anyone but myself, some scraps of paper, various fragments of writing and attempts at keeping diaries, and the like. I hope they will in any event help you to while away such hours as you cannot find a better way of spending. I leave it to you to judge the proper time for giving my sons the key of the room and for helping them to understand the truth about me. It is important to me that they should know what sort of person their father was – if that is at all possible. I am not concerned that they should think well of me. To be thought well of is the last thing I'm after; but perhaps it would help them to know the truth about themselves, at a time when such knowledge would not be dangerous. If they grow up imbued with the air of this village, its smells and colours and history, the faces of its inhabitants and the memories of its floods and harvestings and sowings, then my life will acquire its true perspective as something meaningful alongside many other meanings of deeper significance. I don't know how they will think of me then. They may feel pity for me or they may, in their imagination, transform me into a hero. That is not important. The important thing is that my life should not emerge from behind the unknown like an evil spirit and cause them harm. How I would have liked to stay on with them, watching them grow up before my eyes and at least constituting some justification for my existence. I do not know which of the two courses would be the more selfish, to stay on or to depart. In any event I have no choice, and perhaps you will realize what I mean if you cast your mind back to what I said to you that night. It's futile to deceive oneself. That distant call still rings in my ears. I thought that my life and marriage here would silence it. But perhaps I was created thus, or my fate was thus – whatever may be the meaning of that I don't know. Rationally I know what is right: my attempt at living in this village with these happy people. But mysterious things in my soul and in my blood impel me towards faraway parts that loom up before me and cannot be ignored. How sad it would be if either or both of my sons grew up with the germ of this infection in them, the wanderlust. I charge you with the trust because I have glimpsed in you a likeness to your grandfather. I don't know when I shall go, my friend, but I sense that the hour of departure has drawn nigh, so good-bye.'

If Mustafa Sa'eed had chosen his end, then he had undertaken the most melodramatic act in the story of his life. If the other possibility was the right one, then Nature had bestowed upon him the very end which he would have wanted for himself. Imagine: the height of summer in the month of fateful July; the indifferent river has flooded as never before in thirty years; the darkness has fused all the elements of nature into one single neutral one, older than the river itself and more indifferent. In such manner the end of this hero had to be. But was it really the end he was looking for? Perhaps he wanted it to happen in the north, the far north, on a stormy, icy night, under a starless sky, among a people to whom he did not matter – the end of conquering invaders. But, as he said, they conspired against him, the jurors and the witnesses and the lawyers and the judges, to deprive him of it. 'The jurors,' he said, 'saw before them a man who didn't want to defend himself,

a man who had lost the desire for life. I hesitated that night when Jean sobbed into my ear, "Come with me. Come with me." My life achieved completion that night and there was no justification for staying on. But I hesitated and at the critical moment I was afraid. I was hoping that the court would grant me what I had been incapable of accomplishing. It was as though, realizing what I was after, they decided that they would not grant me the final request I had of them – even Colonel Hammond who I thought wished me well. He mentioned my visit to them in Liverpool and what a good impression I had made on him. He said that he regarded himself as a liberal person with no prejudices. Yet he was a realistic man and had seen that such a marriage would not work. He said too that his daughter Ann had fallen under the influence of Eastern philosophies at Oxford and that she was hesitating between embracing Buddhism or Islam. He could not say for sure whether her suicide was due to some spiritual crisis or because of finding out that Mr Mustafa Sa'eed had deceived her. Ann was his only daughter, and I had got to know her when she was not yet twenty; I deceived her, seducing her by telling her that we would marry and that our marriage would be a bridge between north and south, and I turned to ashes the firebrand of curiosity in her green eyes. And yet her father stands up in court and says in a calm voice that he can't be sure. This is justice, the rules of the game, like the laws of combat and neutrality in war. This is cruelty that wears the mask of mercy . . .'
The long and short of it is they sentence him to imprisonment, a mere seven years, refusing to take

the decision which he should have taken of his own free will. On coming out of prison he wanders from place to place, from Paris to Copenhagen to Delhi to Bangkok, as he tries to put off the decision. And after that the end came in an obscure village on the Nile; whether it was by chance or whether the curtain was lowered of his own free will no one can say for certain.

But I have not come here to think about Mustafa Sa'eed, for here, craning their necks in front of us, are the closely-packed village houses, made of mud and green bricks, while our donkeys press forward as their nostrils breathe in the scent of clover, fodder, and water. These houses are on the perimeter of the desert: it is as though some people in the past had wanted to settle here and had then washed their hands of it and quickly journeyed away. Here things begin and things end. A small girdle of cold, fresh breeze, amidst the meridional heat of the desert, comes from the direction of the river like a half-truth amidst a world filled with lies. The voices of people, birds and animals expire weakly on the ear like whispers, and the regular puttering of the water pump heightens the sensation of the impossible. And the river, the river but for which there would have been no beginning and no end, flows northwards, pays heed to nothing; a mountain may stand in its way so it turns eastwards; it may happen upon a deep depression so it turns westwards, but sooner or later it settles down in its irrevocable journey towards the sea in the north.

I stood at the door of my grandfather's house in the morning, a vast and ancient door made of harraz, a door that had doubtless been fashioned from the wood of a whole tree. Wad Baseer had made it; Wad Baseer, the village engineer who, though he had not even learnt carpentry at school, had yet made the wheels and rings of the water-wheels, had set bones, had cauterized people and bled with cupping glasses. He was also so knowledgeable about judging donkeys that seldom did anyone from the village buy one without consulting him. Though Wad Baseer is still alive today, he no longer makes such doors as that of my grandfather's house, later generations of villagers having found out about zan wood doors and iron doors which they bring in from Omdurman. The market for water-wheels, too, dried up with the coming of pumps. I heard them guffawing with laughter and made out the thin, mischievous laugh of my grandfather when in a good humour; Wad Rayyes's laugh that issues forth from an ever-full stomach; Bakri's that takes its hue and flavour from the company in which he happens to be; and the strong, mannish laugh of Bint Majzoub. In my mind's eye I see my grandfather sitting on his prayer-mat with his string of sandalwood prayer-beads in his hand revolving in ever-constant movement like the buckets of a water-wheel; Bint

Majzoub, Wad Rayyes and Bakri, all old friends of his, will be sitting on those low couches which are a mere two hand-spans off the floor. According to my grandfather, a couch raised high off the floor indicates vanity, a low one humility. Bint Majzoub will be leaning on one elbow, while in her other hand she holds a cigarette. Wad Rayyes will be giving the impression of producing stories from the tips of his moustaches. Bakri will merely be sitting. This large house is built neither of stone nor yet of red brick but of the very mud in which the wheat is grown, and it stands right at the edge of the field so that it is an extension of it. This is evident from the acacia and sunt bushes that are growing in the courtyard and from the plants that sprout from the very walls where the water has seeped through from the culti-vated land. It is a chaotic house, built without method, and has acquired its present form over many years: many differently-sized rooms, some built up against one another at different times, either because they were needed or because my grandfather found himself with some spare money for which he had no other use. Some of the rooms lead off one another, others have doors so low that you have to double up to enter, yet others are doorless; some have many windows, some none. The walls are smooth and plastered with a mixture of rough sand, black mud and animal dung, likewise the roofs, while the ceilings are of acacia wood and palm-tree trunks and stalks. A maze of a house, cool in summer, warm in winter; if one looks objectively at it from outside one feels it to be a frail structure, incapable of survival, but somehow, as if by a miracle, it has surmounted time.

Entering by the door of the spacious courtyard, I looked to right and to left. Over there were dates spread out on straw matting to dry; over there onions and chillies; over there sacks of wheat and beans, some with mouths stitched up, others open. In a corner a goat eats barley and suckles her young. The fate of this house is bound up with that of the field: if the field waxes green so does it, if drought sweeps over the field it also sweeps over the house. I breathe in that smell peculiar to my grandfather's house, a discordant mixture of onions and chillies and dates and wheat and horse-beans and fenugreek, in addition to the aroma of the incense which is always floating up from the large earthenware censer. The aroma of incense puts me in mind of my grandfather's ascetic manner of life and the luxury of his accessories for prayers: the rug on which he prays, made up of three leopard skins stitched together, and which he would use as a coverlet when it turned excessively cold; the brass ewer with its decorations and inscriptions, which he used for his ablutions, and the matching brass basin. He was especially proud of his sandalwood prayer-beads, which he would run through his fingers and rub against his face, breathing in their aroma; when he got angry with one of his grandchildren he would strike him across the head with them, saying that this would chase away the devil that had got into him. All these things, like the rooms of his house and the date palms in his field, had their own histories which my grandfather had recounted to me time and time again, on each occasion omitting or adding something.

I lingered by the door as I savoured that agreeable sensation which precedes the moment of meeting my grandfather whenever I return from a journey: a sensation of pure astonishment that that ancient being is still in actual existence upon the earth's surface. When I embrace him I breathe in his unique smell which is a combination of the smell of the large mausoleum in the cemetery and the smell of an infant child. And that thin tranquil voice sets up a bridge between me and the anxious moment that has not yet been formed, and between the moments the events of which have been assimilated and have passed on, have become bricks in an edifice with perspectives and dimensions. By the standards of the European industrial world we are poor peasants, but when I embrace my grandfather I experience a sense of richness as though I am a note in the heart-beats of the very universe. He is no towering oak tree with luxuriant branches growing in a land on which Nature has bestowed water and fertility, rather is he like the sayal bushes in the deserts of the Sudan, thick of bark and sharp of thorn, defeating death because they ask so little of life. That was the cause for wonder: that he was actually alive, despite plague and famines, wars and the corruption of rulers. And now here he is nearing his hundredth year. All his teeth are still intact; though you would think his small lustreless eyes were sightless, yet he can see with them in the pitch darkness of night; his body, small and shrunken in upon itself is all bones, veins, skin and muscle, with not a single scrap of fat. None the less he can spring nimbly on to his donkey and walks from his house to the mosque in the twilight of dawn.

My grandfather used the edge of his gown to wipe away the tears that had run down his face from laughing so much, and after giving me time to settle myself in the gathering, said, 'By God, that's some story of yours, Wad Rayyes.' This was a cue to Wad Rayyes to continue the story my entrance had interrupted. 'And afterwards, Hajj Ahmed, I put the girl in front of me on the donkey, squirming and twisting, then I forcibly stripped her of all her clothes till she was as naked as the day her mother bore her. She was a young slave girl from down-river who'd just reached puberty – her breasts, Hajj Ahmed, stuck out like pistols and your arms wouldn't meet round her buttocks. She had been rubbed all over with oil so that her skin glistened in the moonlight and her perfume turned one giddy. I took her down to a sandy patch in the middle of the maize, but when I started on her I heard a movement in the maize and a voice saying, "Who's there?" O Hajj Ahmed, there's no madness like the madness of youth. Thinking quickly, I made out I was an afreet and began letting out fiendish shrieks, scattering sand around and stamping about, so the man panicked and fled. The joke was, though, that my uncle Isa had been following hard on my heels from the moment I snatched the girl from the wedding house right up to when we arrived at the patch of sand. When he saw I was pretending to be an afreet, he stood by watching. Early the next day he went off to my father, may God rest his soul, and told him the

74

whole story. "This son of yours is a real devil," he told him, "and if you don't find him a wife this very day he'll corrupt the whole village and bring down on us no end of scandals," and they in fact married me off that very day to my uncle Rajab's daughter. God rest her soul, she died giving birth to her first child. "Since when," said Bint Majzoub to him, laughing in her manly voice made hoarse by too much smoking, "you've been jumping on and off like a jack donkey."

"'Is there anyone who knows the sweetness of this thing better than you, Bint Majzoub?" Wad Rayyes said to her. "You've buried eight husbands and now you're an old woman you wouldn't say no if you were offered it."

"'We've heard," said my grandfather, "that Bint Majzoub's cries of delight had to be heard to be believed."

"'May I divorce, Hajj Ahmed," said Bint Majzoub, lighting up a cigarette," if when my husband was between my thighs I didn't let out a scream that used to scare the animals tied up at pasture."

'Bakri, who previously had been laughing without saying anything, said, "Tell us, Bint Majzoub, which of your husbands was the best?"

"'Wad Basheer," said Bint Majzoub promptly.

"'Wad Basheer the dozy dope," said Bakri. "He was so slow a goat could make off with his supper."

"'May I divorce," said Bint Majzoub, freeing the ash from her cigarette on to the ground with a theatrical movement of her fingers, "if his thing wasn't like a wedge he'd drive right into me so I could hardly contain myself. He'd lift up my legs

75

after the evening prayer and I'd remain splayed open till the call to prayers at dawn. When he had his climax he'd shout like an ox being slaughtered, and always when moving from on top of me he would say, 'Praise be to God, Bint Majzoub.'"

"'It's not surprising you killed him off in the bloom of youth,'' said my grandfather to her.

"'The time that fate decreed for him killed him,'' said Bint Majzoub with a laugh. "This business never kills anyone.'"

Bint Majzoub was a tall woman of a charcoal complexion like black velvet who, despite the fact she was approaching seventy, still retained vestiges of beauty. She was famous in the village, and men and women alike were eager to listen to her conversation which was daring and uninhibited. She used to smoke, drink and swear on oath of divorce like a man. It was said that her mother was the daughter of one of the Fur sultans in Darfur. She had been married to a number of the leading men of the village, all of whom had died and left her a considerable fortune. She had borne one son and a countless number of daughters who were famous for their beauty and for being as uninhibited in their conversation as their mother. It was recounted that one of Bint Majzoub's daughters married a man of whom her mother did not approve. He took her off on a journey with him and on his return about a year later he decided to hold a banquet to which to invite his wife's relatives. 'My mother is quite uninhibited in the way she talks,' the wife said to him, 'and it would be better to invite her on her own.' So they slaughtered some animals and invited her along. After she had eaten and drunk Bint Majzoub said to her daughter, in her husband's hearing, 'Amna, this man has not done badly by you, for your house is beautiful and so is your clothing, and he has filled your hands and neck with gold. However it would not appear from the look of him that he is able to satisfy you in bed. Now if you want to have real satisfaction I can find you a husband who once he mounts you will not get off till you're at your last gasp.' When the husband heard these words he was so angry he divorced his wife irrevocably on the spot.

'What's come over you?' Bint Majzoub said to Wad Rayyes. 'For two years now you've contented yourself with a single wife. Has your prowess waned?'

Wad Rayyes and my grandfather exchanged glances the meaning of which I was to understand only later. 'The face is that of an old man, the heart that of a young one,' said Wad Rayyes. 'Do you know of a widow or divorced woman who would suit me?'

'By God, the truth is, Wad Rayyes,' said Bakri, 'that you're past marrying again. You're now an old man in your seventies and your grandchildren have children of their own. Aren't you ashamed of yourself having a wedding every year? What you need now is to bear yourself with dignity and prepare to meet the Almighty God.'

Bint Majzoub and my grandfather both laughed at these words. 'What do you understand of these matters?' said Wad Rayyes in feigned anger. 'Both you and Hajj Ahmed made do with one woman, and when they died and left you you couldn't find the courage to marry again. Hajj Ahmed here spends all day praying and telling his beads as though Paradise had been created just for him. And you, Bakri, busy yourself in making money till death gives you release from it. Almighty God sanctioned marriage and He sanctioned divorce. "Take them with liberality and separate from them with liberality," he said. "Women and children are the adornment of life on this earth," God said in His noble Book.'

I said to Wad Rayyes that the Koran did not say 'Women and children' but 'Wealth and children'.

He answered: 'In any case, there's no pleasure like that of fornication.'

Wad Rayyes carefully stroked his curved moustaches upwards, their ends like needle-points, then with his left hand began rubbing the thick white beard that covered his face right up to his temples. Its utter whiteness contrasted strongly with the brownness of his skin, the colour of tanned leather, so that his beard looked like something artificial stuck on to his face. However, the whiteness of his beard blended without difficulty with the whiteness of his large turban, forming a striking frame that brought out the main features of his face: the beautifully intelligent eyes and the thin elegant nose. Wad Rayyes used kohl on his eyes: though he gave as his reason for so doing the fact that kohl was enjoined in the sunna, I believe it was out of vanity. It was in its entirety a beautiful face, especially if you compared it to that of my grandfather, which had nothing characteristic about it, or with Bakri's which was like a wrinkled water melon. It was obvious that Wad Rayyes was aware of this. I heard that in his youth he was a strikingly handsome man and that the girls, south and north, up-river and down, lost their hearts to him. He had been much married and much divorced, taking no heed of anything in a woman except that she was woman, taking them as they came, and if asked about it replying, 'A stallion isn't finicky.' I remember that among his wives was a Dongola woman from El-Khandak, a Hadandawi woman from El-Gedaref, an Abyssinian he'd found employed as a servant by his eldest son in Khartoum, and a woman from Nigeria he'd brought back with him from his fourth pilgrimage. When asked how he had married her he said he'd met her and her husband on the ship between Port Sudan and Jeddah and that he'd struck up a friendship with them. The man, however, had died in Mecca on the Day of Halting at Arafat and had said to him as he was dying, 'I ask you to look well after my wife.' He could think of no way of looking after her better than by marrying her, and she lived with him for three years which, for Wad Rayyes, was a long time. He had been delighted with her, the greater part of his pleasure coming from the fact that she was barren. Recounting to people the details of his intimacies with her, he would say, 'No one who hasn't been married to a Nigerian knows what marriage is.' During his time with her he married a woman from the Kababeesh he brought back with him from a visit to Hamrat El-Sheikh, but the two women could not bear living together so he divorced the Nigerian to please the Kababeeshi woman, who after a while deserted him and fled to her people in Hamrat El-Sheikh.

Wad Rayyes prodded me in the side with his elbow and said, 'They say the infidel women are something unbelievable.'

'I wouldn't know,' I said to him.

'What a way to talk!' he said. 'A young lad like you in the flower of his youth spending seven years in the land of hanky-panky and you say you don't know.'

I was silent and Wad Rayyes said, 'This tribe of yours isn't any good. You're one-woman men. The only real man among you is Abdul Karim. Now there's a man for you.'

We were in fact known in the village for not divorcing our wives and for not having more than one. The villagers used to joke about us and say that we were afraid of our women, except for my uncle Abdul Karim who was both much divorced and much married – and an adulterer to boot.

'The infidel women aren't so knowledgeable about this business as our village girls,' said Bint Majzoub. 'They're uncircumcized and treat the whole business like having a drink of water. The village girl gets herself rubbed all over with oil and perfumed and puts on a silky night-wrap, and when she lies down on the red mat after the evening prayer and opens her thighs, a man feels like he's Abu Zeid El-Hilali. The man who's not interested perks up and gets interested.'

My grandfather laughed and so did Bakri.

'Enough of you and your local girls,' said Wad

Rayyes. 'The women abroad, they're the or right.'

'Your brain's abroad,' said Bint Majzoub.

'Wad Rayyes likes uncircumcised women,' said my grandfather.

'I swear to you, Hajj Ahmed,' said Wad Rayyes, 'that if you'd had a taste of the women of Abyssinia and Nigeria you'd throw away your string of prayer-beads and give up praying – the thing between their thighs is like an upturned dish, all there for good or bad. We here lop it off and leave it like a piece of land that's been stripped bare.'

'Circumcision is one of the conditions of Islam,' said Bakri.

'What Islam are you talking about?' asked Wad Rayyes. 'It's your Islam and Hajj Ahmed's Islam, because you can't tell what's good for you from what's bad. The Nigerians, the Egyptians, and the Arabs of Syria, aren't they Moslems like us? But they're people who know what's what and leave their women as God created them. As for us, we dock them like you do animals.'

My grandfather laughed so hard that three beads from his string slipped by together without his realizing. 'As for Egyptian women, the likes of you aren't up to them,' he said.

'And what do you know of Egyptian women?' Wad Rayyes said to him. Replying for my grandfather, Bakri said, 'Have you forgotten that Hajj Ahmed travelled to Egypt in the year six* and stayed there for nine months?'

* i.e. 1306 of the Hegira, or Moslem Calendar, which starts in 622 A.D.

'I walked there,' said my grandfather, 'with nothing but my string of prayer-beads and my ewer.'

'And what did you do?' said Wad Rayyes. 'Return as you went, with your string of beads and your ewer? I swear to you that if I'd been in your place I wouldn't have come back empty-handed.'

'I believe you'd have come back with a woman,' said my grandfather. 'That's all you worry about. I returned with money with which to buy land, repair the water-wheel, and circumcise my sons.'

'Good God, Hajj Ahmed, didn't you taste a bit of the Egyptian stuff?' said Wad Rayyes.

The prayer-beads were slipping through my grandfather's fingers all this time, up and down like a water-wheel. The movement suddenly ceased and my grandfather raised his face to the ceiling and opened his mouth, but Bakri beat him to it and said, 'Wad Rayyes, you're mad. You're old in years but you've got no sense. Women are women whether they're in Egypt, the Sudan, Iraq or the land of Mumbo-jumbo. The black, the white, and the red – they're all one and the same.'

So great was his astonishment that Wad Rayyes was unable to say anything. He looked at Bint Majzoub as though appealing to her for help. 'In God's truth, I almost got married in Egypt,' said my grandfather. 'The Egyptians are good, God-fearing people, and the Egyptian woman knows how to respect a man. I got to know a man in Boulak – we used to meet up for dawn prayers in the Abu 'l-Ala Mosque. I was invited to his house and got to know his family. He was the father of several daughters – six of them and any of them was beautiful enough to be able to say to the moon "Get down and I'll sit in your place". After some time he said to me, "O Sudanese, you are a religious and God-fearing man, let me give you one of my daughters in marriage." In God's truth, Wad Rayyes, I really fancied the eldest, but shortly after this I got a telegram telling me of my late mother's death, so I left then and there.'

'May God rest her soul,' said Bakri. 'She was a fine woman.' Wad Rayyes gave a deep sigh and said, 'What a pity – that's life though. It gives to those who don't want to take. I swear to you if I'd been in your place I'd have done all sorts of things. I'd have married and settled there and tasted the sweetness of life with the Egyptian girls. What brought you back to this barren, good-for-nothing place?'

'The gazelle said, "To me my desert country is as beautiful as Syria"', Bakri quoted the proverb.

Lighting up another cigarette and drawing strongly on it so that the air in the room was clouded, Bint Majzoub said to Wad Rayyes, 'You're not deprived of the sweetness of life even in this barren, good-for-nothing place. Here you are, hail and hearty and growing no older though you're over seventy.'

'I swear, a mere seventy only, not a day older, though *you're* a good deal older than Hajj Ahmed.'

'Have a fear of God, Wad Rayyes!' my grandfather said to him. 'Bint Majzoub wasn't born when I married. She's two or three years younger than you.'

'In any event,' said Wad Rayyes, 'as we stand today, I'm the most energetic one of you. And I'll swear that when I'm between a woman's thighs I'm more energetic than even this grandson of yours.'

'You're a great one for talking,' said Bint Majzoub. 'You doubtless run after women because what you've got to offer is no bigger than a finger-joint.'

'If only you'd married me, Bint Majzoub,' said Wad Rayyes, 'you'd have found something like a British cannon.'

'The cannon were silenced when Wad Basheer died,' said Bint Majzoub. 'Wad Rayyes, you're a man who talks rubbish. Your whole brain's in the head of your penis and the head of your penis is as small as your brain.'

Their voices were all raised in laughter, even that of Bakri who had previously laughed quietly. My grandfather ceased altogether clicking his prayer-beads and gave his thin, shrill, mischievous laugh. Bint Majzoub laughed in her hoarse, manly voice, while Wad Rayyes's laugh was more of a snort than a laugh.

As they wiped the tears from their eyes, my grandfather said, 'I ask forgiveness of Almighty God, I pray pardon of Him.'

'I ask forgiveness of Almighty God,' said Bint Majzoub. 'By God, what a laugh we've had. May God bring us together again on some auspicious occasion.'

'I ask God's forgiveness,' said Bakri. 'May God do as He wishes with us all the days of our lives on this earth and in the Hereafter.'

'I ask forgiveness of God,' said Wad Rayyes.

'We spend our days on the face of the earth and in
the Hereafter God does with us as He wills.'

Bint Majzoub sprang to her feet at a bound like a
man in his thirties and stood up perfectly straight,
with no curve to her back or bend to her shoulders.
As though bearing some weight, Bakri stood up.
Wad Rayyes rose, leaning slightly on his stick. My
grandfather got up from his prayer-rug and seated
himself on the couch with the short legs. I looked at
them: three old men and an old woman laughing a
while as they stood at the grave's edge. Tomorrow
they would be on their way. Tomorrow the grandson would become a father, the father a grandfather,
and the caravan would pass on.

Then they left. 'Tomorrow, Effendi, you're
lunching with us,' Wad Rayyes said to me as he was
going.

My grandfather stretched himself out on the
couch, then laughed, alone this time, as though to
underline his feeling of isolation, after the departure
of the people who had made him laugh and whom
he had made laugh. After a while he said, 'Do you
know why Wad Rayyes invited you to lunch?' I
told him we were friends and that he had invited me
before. 'He wants a favour of you,' said my grandfather.

'What's he want?' I said.

'He wants to get married,' he said.

I made a show of laughing and asked my grandfather what Wad Rayyes's marrying had to do with
me.

'You're the bride's guardian.'

I took refuge in silence and my grandfather,

85

nking I had not understood, said, 'Wad Rayyes
.ants to marry Mustafa Sa'eed's widow.'
Again I took refuge in silence. 'Wad Rayyes is
sprightly enough – and he's got money,' said my
grandfather. 'In any case, the woman needs someone
to protect her. Three years have passed since her
husband's death. Doesn't she ever want to re-
marry?'

I told him I was not responsible for her. There was
her father, her brothers, why didn't Wad Rayyes ask
for her from them?

'The whole village knows,' said my grandfather,
'that Mustafa Sa'eed made you guardian of his wife
and children.'

I told him that while I was guardian of the children the wife was free to do as she pleased and she
was not without relatives. 'She listens to what you
say,' said my grandfather. 'If you were to talk to her
she might agree.'

I felt real anger, which astonished me for such
things are commonly done in the village. 'She has
refused younger men than him,' I said to my grandfather. 'He's forty years older than her.' However,
my grandfather insisted that Wad Rayyes was still
sprightly, that he was comfortably off and that he
was sure her father would not oppose it; however,
the woman herself might refuse and so they had
wanted to make a persuasive intermediary out of me.

Anger checked my tongue and I kept silent. The
obscene pictures sprang simultaneously to my
mind, and, to my extreme astonishment, the two
pictures merged: I imagined Hosna Bint Mahmoud,
Mustafa Sa'eed's widow, as being the same woman
86

in both instances: two white, wide-open thighs in London, and a woman groaning before dawn in an obscure village on a bend of the Nile under the weight of the aged Wad Rayyes. If that other thing was evil, this too was evil, and if this was like death and birth, the Nile flood and the wheat harvest, a part of the system of the universe, so too was that. I pictured Hosna Bint Mahmoud, Mustafa Sa'eed's widow, a woman in her thirties, weeping under seventy-year-old Wad Rayyes. Her weeping would be made the subject of one of Wad Rayyes's famous stories about his many women with which he regales the men of the village. The rage in my breast grew more savage. Unable to remain, I left; behind me I heard my grandfather calling but I did not turn round.

At home my father inquired of me the reason for my bad humour so I told him the story. 'Is that something to get angry about?' he said, laughing.

At approximately four o'clock in the afternoon I went to Mustafa Sa'eed's house. I entered by the door of the large courtyard, glanced momentarily to the left at the rectangular room of red brick, silent not as the grave but as a ship that has cast anchor in mid-ocean. However, the time had not yet come. She sat me down in a chair on the stone stoop outside the *diwan* – the very same place – and brought me a glass of lemon juice. The two boys came up and paid their respects to me; the elder was called Mahmoud, her father's name, and the younger Sa'eed, his father's name. They were ordinary children, one eight and the other seven, who went off each morning to their school six miles away seated one behind the other on a donkey. They are my responsibility, and one of the reasons that brings me here each year is to see how they are getting on. This time we shall be holding their circumcision ceremony and shall bring along professional singers and religious chanters to a celebration that will be a landmark in their childhood memories. He had told me to spare them the pangs of wanderlust. I would do nothing of the sort; when they grew up, if they wanted to travel, they should be allowed to. Everyone starts at the beginning of the road, and the world is in an endless state of childhood.

The two boys left and she remained, standing in

front of me: a slim, tallish figure, firmly built and as lithe as a length of sugar cane; while she used no henna on her feet or hands, a slight smell of perfume hung about her. Her lips were naturally dark red and her teeth strong, white and even. She had a handsome face with wide black eyes in which sadness mingled with shyness. When I greeted her I felt her hand soft and warm in mine. She was a woman of noble carriage and of a foreign type of beauty – or am I imagining something that is not really there? A woman for whom, when I meet her, I feel a sense of hazard and constraint so that I flee from her as quickly as I can. This woman is the offering Wad Rayyes wants to sacrifice at the edge of the grave, with which to bribe death and so gain a respite of a year or two.

She remained standing despite my insistence and only seated herself when I said to her, 'if you don't sit down I'll go.' Conversation began slowly and with difficulty, and thus it continued while the sun sank down towards its place of setting and little by little the air grew cooler and little by little our tongues loosened. I said something that made her laugh and my heart throbbed at the sweetness of her laughter. The blood of the setting sun suddenly spilled out on the western horizon like that of millions of people who have died in some violent war that has broken out between Earth and Heaven. Suddenly the war ended in defeat and a complete and all-embracing darkness descended and pervaded all four corners of the globe, wiping out the sadness and shyness that was in her eyes. Nothing remained but the voice warmed by affection, and the faint me which was like a spring that might dry up at any moment.

'Did you love Mustafa Sa'eed?' I suddenly asked her.

She did not answer. Though I waited a while she still did not answer. Then I realized that the darkness and the perfume were all but causing me to lose control and that mine was not a question to be asked at such a time and place.

However, it was not long before her voice breached a gap in the darkness and broke through to my ear. 'He was the father of my children.' If I am right in my belief, the voice was not sad, in fact it contained a caressing tenderness. I let the silence whisper to her, hoping she would say something further. Yes, here it was: 'He was a generous husband and a generous father. He never let us want for anything in his whole life.'

'Did you know where he was from?' I said as I leaned towards her in the darkness.

'From Khartoum,' she said.

'And what had he been doing in Khartoum?' I said.

'He'd been in business,' she said.

'And what brought him here?' I said.

'God knows,' she said.

I almost despaired. Then a brisk breeze blew in my direction, carrying a charge of perfume greater than I had hoped for. As I breathed it in I felt my despair becoming keener.

Suddenly a large opening occurred in the darkness through which penetrated a voice, this time a sad one with a sadness deeper than the bottom of the river. 'I think he was hiding something,' she said.

'Why?' I pursued her with the question.

'He used to spend a lot of time at night in that room,' she said.

'What's in that room?' I asked, intensifying my pursuit.

'I don't know,' she said. 'I've never been in it. You have the keys. Why don't you investigate for yourself?'

Yes, supposing we were to get up, she and I, this instant, light the lamp, and enter, would we find him strung up by the neck from the ceiling, or would we find him sitting squat-legged on the floor?

'Why do you think he was hiding something?' I asked her again.

Her voice was not sad now and contained no caressing tenderness; it was saw-edged like a maize leaf.

'Sometimes at night when he was asleep he'd say things in – in gibberish.'

'What gibberish?' I followed up.

'I don't know,' she said. 'It was like European talk.'

I remained leaning forward towards her in the darkness, watching, waiting.

'He kept repeating words in his sleep, like Jeena Jeeny – I don't know.'

In this very place, at just such a time, in just such darkness as this, his voice, like dead fishes floating on the surface of the sea, used to float out. 'I went on pursuing her for three years. Every day the bow string became more taut. My caravans were parched with thirst and the mirage glimmered in front of me in the desert of longing. On that night when Jean whispered in my ear, "Come with me. Come with me," my life had reached completion and there was no reason to stay on –' The shriek of a child reached me from some place in the quarter.

'It was as though he felt his end drawing near,' said Hosna. 'A week before the day – the day before his death – he arranged his affairs. He tidied up odds and ends and paid his debts. The day before he died he called me to him and told me what he owned and gave me numerous directions about the boys. He also gave me the letter sealed with wax and said to me, "Give it to him if anything happens." He told me that if anything happened you were to be the boys' guardian. "Consult him in everything you do," he said to me. I cried and said to him, "God willing, nothing bad will happen." "It's just in case," he said, "for one never knows in this world." That day I implored him not to go down to the field because of all the flooding. I was afraid, but he told me not to be, and that he was a good swimmer. I was apprehensive all day long and my fears increased when he didn't come back at his usual time. We waited and then it happened.'

I was conscious of her crying silently, then her weeping grew louder and was transformed into a fierce sobbing that shook the darkness lying between her and me. Her perfume and the silence were lost and nothing existed in the whole world except the lamentation of a woman for a husband she did not know, for a man who, spreading his sails, had voyaged off on the ocean in pursuit of a foreign mirage. And the old man Wad Rayyes dreams in his house of nights of dalliance under the silken night-wrap. And I, what shall I do now amidst this chaos? Shall I go up to her, clasp her to my breast, dry her tears with my handkerchief and restore serenity to her heart with my words? I half raised myself, leaning on my arm, but I sensed danger as I remembered something, and remained as I was for a time in a state between action and restraint. Suddenly a feeling of heavy weariness assailed me and I sank down on to the chair. The darkness was thick, deep and basic – not a condition in which light was merely absent; the darkness was now constant, as though light had never existed and the stars in the sky were nothing but rents in an old and tattered garment. The perfume was a jumble of dreams, an unheard sound like that of ants' feet in a mound of sand. From the belly of the darkness there issued forth a voice that was not hers, a voice that was neither angry, nor sad, nor frightened, nothing more than a voice saying: 'The lawyers were fighting over my body. It was not I who was important but the case. Professor Maxwell Foster-Keen – one of the founders of the Moral Rearmament movement in Oxford, a Mason, and a member of the Supreme Committee for the Protestant Missionary Societies in Africa – did not conceal his dislike of me. In the days when I was a student of his at Oxford he would say to me with undisguised irritation: "You, Mr Sa'eed, are the best example of the fact that our civilizing mission in Africa is of no avail. After all the efforts we've made to educate you, it's as if you'd come out of the jungle for the first time." And here he was, notwithstanding, employing all his skill to save me from the gallows. Then there was Sir Arthur Higgins, twice married and twice divorced, whose love affairs were notorious and who was famous for his connections with the left and Bohemian circles. I had spent the Christmas of 1925 at his house in Saffron Walden. He used to say to me, "You're a scoundrel, but I don't dislike scoundrels because I'm one myself." Yet in court he employed all his skill to place the hangman's noose around my neck. The jurors, too, were a varied bunch of people and included a labourer, a doctor, a farmer, a teacher, a businessman, and an undertaker, with nothing in common between them and me; had I asked one of them to rent me a room in his house he would as likely as not have refused, and were his daughter to tell him she was going to marry this African, he'd have felt that the world was collapsing under his feet. Yet each one of them in that court would rise above himself for the first time in his life, while I had a sort of feeling of superiority towards them, for the ritual was being held primarily because of me; and I, over and above everything else, am a colonizer, I am the intruder whose fate must be decided. When Mahmoud Wad Ahmed was brought in shackles to Kitchener after his defeat at the Battle of Atbara, Kitchener said to him, "Why have you come to my country to lay waste and plunder?" It was the intruder who said this to the person whose land it was, and the owner of the land bowed his head and said nothing. So let it be with me. In that court I hear the rattle of swords in Carthage and the clatter of the hooves of Allenby's horses desecrating the ground of Jerusalem. The ships at first sailed down the Nile carrying guns not bread, and the railways were originally set up to transport troops; the schools were started so as to teach us how to say "Yes" in their language. They imported to us the germ of the greatest European violence, as seen on the Somme and at Verdun, the like of which the world has never previously known, the germ of a deadly disease that struck them more than a thousand years ago. Yes, my dear sirs, I came as an invader into your very homes: a drop of the poison which you have injected into the veins of history. 'I am no Othello. Othello was a lie.'

Thinking over Mustafa Sa'eed's words as he sat in that very place on just such a night as this, I listened to her sobbing as though it came to me from afar, mingled in my mind with scattered noises which I had no doubt heard at odd times but which all intertwined together in my brain like a carillon of church bells: the scream of a child somewhere in the neighbourhood, the crowing of cocks, the braying of a donkey, and the sounds of a wedding coming from the far side of the river. But now I heard only one sound, that of her anguished weeping. I did nothing. I sat on where I was without moving and left her to weep alone to the night till she stopped. I had to say something, so I said, 'Clinging to the past does no one any good. You have two children and are still a young woman in the prime of life. Think about the future. Who knows, perhaps you will accept one of the numerous suitors who want to marry you.'

'After Mustafa Sa'eed,' she answered immediately,

with a decisiveness that astonished me, 'I shall go to no man.'

Though I had not intended to, I said to her, 'Wad Rayyes wants to marry you. Your father and family don't object. He asked me to talk to you on his behalf.'

She was silent for so long that, presuming she was not going to say anything, I was on the point of getting up to leave. At last, though, I became aware of her voice in the darkness like the blade of a knife. 'If they force me to marry, I'll kill him and kill myself.'

I thought of several things to say, but presently I heard the muezzin calling for the night prayer: 'God is great. God is great'. So I stood up, and so did she, and I left without saying anything.

While I was drinking my morning coffee Wad Rayyes came to me. I had intended to go to his house but he forestalled me. He said that he had come to remind me of the invitation of the day before, but I knew that, unable to hold himself in wait, he had come to learn of the result of my intervention.

'It's no good,' I told him as he seated himself. 'She doesn't want to marry at all. If I were you I'd certainly let the whole matter drop.'

I had not imagined that the news would have such an effect on him. However Wad Rayyes, who changed women as he changed donkeys, now sat in front of me with a morose expression on his face, eyelids trembling, savagely biting his lower lip. He began fidgeting in his seat and tapping the ground nervously with his stick. He took off the slipper from his right foot and put it on again several times as though preparing to get up and go, then reseated himself and opened his mouth as though wishing to speak but without doing so. How extraordinary! Was it reasonable to suppose that Wad Rayyes was in love? 'It's not as if there're not plenty of other women to marry,' I said to him.

His intelligent eyes were no longer intelligent but had become two small glass globes fixed in a rigid stare. 'I shall marry no one but her,' he said. 'She'll accept me whether she likes it or not. Does she imagine she's some queen or princess? Widows in this village are more common than empty bellies. She should thank God she's found a husband like me.'

'If she's just like every other woman, then why this insistence?' I said to him. 'You know she's refused many men besides you, some of them younger. If she wants to devote herself to bringing up her children, why not let her do as she pleases?'

Suddenly Wad Rayyes burst out into a crazy fit of rage which I regarded as quite out of character. In a violent state of excitement, he said something that truly astonished me: 'Ask yourself why Mahmoud's daughter refused marriage. You're the reason – there's certainly something between you and her. Why do you interfere? You're not her father or her brother or the person responsible for her. She'll marry me whatever you or she says or does. Her father's agreed and so have her brothers. This nonsense you learn at school won't wash with us here. In this village the men are guardians of the women.'

I don't know what would have happened if my father had not come in at that moment. Immediately I got up and left.

I went to see Mahjoub in his field. Mahjoub and I are of the same age. We had grown up together and had sat at adjoining desks in the elementary school. He was more clever than I. When we finished our elementary education Mahjoub had said, 'This amount of education will do me – reading, writing and arithmetic. We're farming folk like our fathers and grandfathers. All the education a farmer wants is to be able to write letters, to read the newspapers and to know the prescribed rules for prayers. Also so that if we've got some problem we can make ourselves understood with the powers-that-be.'

I went my own way and Mahjoub turned into a real power in the village, so that today he has become the Chairman of the Agricultural Project Committee and the Co-operative, and a member of the committee of the hospital that is almost finished. He heads every delegation which goes to the provincial centre to take up instances of injustice. With independence Mahjoub became one of the local leaders of the National Democratic Socialist Party. We would occasionally chat about our childhood in the village and he would say to me, 'But look where you are now and where I am. You've become a senior civil servant and I'm a farmer in this god-forsaken village.'

'It's you who've succeeded, not I,' I would say to him with genuine admiration, 'because you influence actual life in the country. We civil servants, though, are of no consequence. People like you are the legal heirs of authority; you are the sinews of life, you're the salt of the earth.'

'If we're the salt of the earth,' Mahjoub would say with a laugh, 'then the earth is without flavour.'

He laughed too on hearing of my encounter with Wad Rayyes. 'Wad Rayyes is an old windbag. He doesn't mean what he says.'

'You know that my relationship with her is dictated by duty, neither more nor less,' I said to him.

'Don't pay any attention to Wad Rayyes's drivel,' said Mahjoub. 'Your reputation in the village is without blemish. The people all speak well of you because you're doing your duty by the children of Mustafa Sa'eed, God rest his soul. He was, after all, a stranger who was in no way related to you.' After a short silence he said, 'Anyway if the woman's father and brothers are agreeable no one can do anything about it.'

'But if she doesn't want to marry?' I said to him.

'You know how life is run here,' he interrupted me. 'Women belong to men, and a man's a man even if he's decrepit.'

'But the world's changed,' I said to him. 'These are things that no longer fit in with our life in this age.'

'The world hasn't changed as much as you think,' said Mahjoub. 'Some things have changed – pumps instead of water-wheels, iron ploughs instead of wooden ones, sending our daughters to school, radios, cars, learning to drink whisky and beer instead of arak and millet wine – yet even so everything's as it was.' Mahjoub laughed as he said, 'The world will really have changed when the likes of me become ministers in the government. And naturally that,' he added still laughing, 'is an out-and-out impossibility.'

'Do you think Wad Rayyes has fallen in love with Hosna Bint Mahmoud?' I said to Mahjoub, who had cheered me up.

'It's not out of the question,' said Mahjoub. 'Wad Rayyes is a man who hankers after things. For two years now he's been singing her praises. He asked for her in marriage before and her father accepted but she refused. They waited, hoping that in time she'd accept.'

'But why this sudden passion?" I said to Mahjoub. 'Wad Rayyes has known Hosna Bint Mahmoud since she was a child. Do you remember her as a wild young girl climbing trees and fighting with boys? As a child she used to swim naked with us in the river. What's happened to change that now?'

'Wad Rayyes,' said Mahjoub, 'is like one of those people who are crazy about owning donkeys – he only admires a donkey when he sees some other man riding it. Only then does he find it beautiful and strives hard to buy it, even if he has to pay more than it's worth.' After thinking for a while in silence, he said, 'It's true, though, that Mahmoud's daughter changed after her marriage to Mustafa Sa'eed. All women change after marriage, but she in particular underwent an indescribable change. It was as though she were another person. Even we who were her contemporaries and used to play with her in the village look at her today and see her as something new – like a city woman, if you know what I mean.'

I asked Mahjoub about Mustafa Sa'eed. 'God rest his soul,' he said. 'We had a mutual respect for each other. At first the relationship between us was not a strong one, but our work together on the Project Committee brought us closer. His death was an irreparable loss. You know, he gave us invaluable help in organizing the Project. He used to look after the accounts and his business experience was of great use to us. It was he who pointed out that we should invest the profits from the Project in setting up a flour mill. We were saved a lot of expense and today people come to us from all over the place. It was he too who pointed out that we should open a co-operative shop. Our prices now are no higher than those in Khartoum. In the old days, as you know, supplies used to arrive by steamer once or twice a month. The traders would hoard them till the market had run out, then they would sell them for many times their cost. Today the Project owns ten lorries that bring us supplies every other day direct from Khartoum and Omdurman. I asked him more than once to take over the Chairmanship, but he always used to refuse, saying I was better suited. The Omda and the merchants absolutely loathed him because he opened the villagers' eyes and spoiled things for them. After his death there were rumours that they had planned to kill him – mere talk. He died from drowning – tens of men were drowned that year. He was a man of great mental capacity. Now, there was a man – if there is any justice in the world – who deserved to be a minister in the government.'

'Politics have spoilt you,' I said to Mahjoub. 'You've come to think only in terms of power. Let's not talk about ministries and the government – tell me about him as a man. What sort of a person was he?'

Astonishment showed on his face. 'What do you mean by what sort of a person?' he said. 'He was as I've described him.' I could not find the appropriate words for explaining what I meant to Mahjoub. 'In any case,' he said, 'what's the reason for your interest in Mustafa Sa'eed? You've already asked me several times about him.' Before I could reply Mahjoub continued, 'You know, I don't understand why he made you the guardian of his children. Of course, you deserve the honour of the trust and have carried our your responsibilities in admirable fashion. Yet you knew him less than any of us. We were here with him in the village while you saw him only from year to year. I was expecting he'd have made me, or your grandfather, guardian. Your grandfather was a close friend of his and he used to enjoy listening to his conversation. He used to say to me, "You know, Mahjoub, Hajj Ahmed is a unique person." "Hajj Ahmed's an old windbag," I would reply and he would get really annoyed. "No, don't say that," he'd say to me. "Hajj Ahmed is a part of history."'

'In any case,' I said to Mahjoub. 'I'm only a

guardian in name. The real guardian is you. The two boys are here with you, and I'm way off in Khartoum.'

'They're intelligent and well-mannered boys,' said Mahjoub. 'They take after their father. They couldn't be doing better in their studies.'

'What will happen to them,' I said, 'if this laughable business of marriage Wad Rayyes has in mind goes through?'

'Take it easy!' said Mahjoub. 'Wad Rayyes will certainly become obsessed with some other woman. Let's suppose, at the very worst, she marries him; I don't think he'll live more than a year or two, and she'll have her share of his many lands and crops.'

Then, like a sudden blow that lands right on the top of one's head, Mahjoub's words struck home: 'Why don't *you* marry her?' My heart beat so violently within me that I almost lost control. It was some time before I found words and, in a trembling voice, said to Mahjoub: 'You're joking of course.'

'Seriously,' he said, 'why don't you marry her? I'm certain she'd accept. You're the guardian of the two boys, and you might as well round things off by becoming a father.'

I remembered her perfume of the night before and the thoughts about her that had taken root in my head in the darkness.

'Don't tell me,' I heard Mahjoub saying with a laugh, 'that you're already a husband and a father. Every day men are taking second wives. You wouldn't be the first or the last.'

'You're completely mad,' I said to Mahjoub, laughing, having recovered my self-control.

I left him and took myself off, having become certain about a fact which was later on to cost me much peace of mind: that in one form or another I was in love with Hosna Bint Mahmoud, the widow of Mustafa Sa'eed, and that I – like him and Wad Rayyes and millions of others – was not immune from the germ of contagion that oozes from the body of the universe.

in love
  with Hosna

After we had had the circumcision celebrations for the two boys I returned to Khartoum. Leaving my wife and daughter in the village, I journeyed by the desert road in one of the Project's lorries. I generally used to travel by steamer to the river port of Karima and from there I would take the train, passing by Abu Hamad and Atbara to Khartoum. But this time I was, for no particular reason, in a hurry, so I chose to go the shortest way. The lorry set off first thing in the morning and proceeded eastwards along the Nile for about two hours, then turned southwards at right angles and struck off into the desert. There is no shelter from the sun which rises up into the sky with unhurried steps, its rays spilling out on the ground as though there existed an old blood feud between it and the people of the earth. There is no shelter apart from the hot shade inside the lorry – shade that is not really shade. A monotonous road rises and falls with nothing to entice the eye: scattered bushes in the desert, all thorns and leafless, miserable trees that are neither alive nor dead. The lorry travels for hours without our coming across a single human being or animal. Then it passes by a herd of camels, likewise lean and emaciated. There is not a single cloud heralding hope in this hot sky which is like the lid of Hell-fire. The day here is something without value, a

mere torment suffered by living creatures as they
await the night. Night is deliverance. In a state close
to fever, haphazard thoughts flooded through my
head: words taken from sentences, the forms of
faces, voices which all sounded as desiccated as light
flurries of wind blowing across fallow fields. Why
the hurry? 'Why the hurry?' she had asked me. 'Why
don't you stay another week?' she had said. 'The
black donkey, a bedouin fellow cheated your uncle
and sold him the black donkey.'

'Is that something to get angry about?' said my
father. Man's mind is not kept in a refrigerator. It is
this sun which is unbearable. It melts the brain. It
paralyses thought. And Mustafa Sa'eed's face springs
clearly to my mind, just as I saw it the first day,
and is then lost in the roar of the lorry's engine
and the sound of the tyres against the desert
stones, and I strive to bring it back and am unable
to.

The day the boys' circumcision was celebrated,
Hosna bared her head and danced as a mother does
on the day her sons are circumcised. What a woman
she is! Why don't *you* marry her? In what manner
used Isabella Seymour to whisper caressingly to
him? 'Ravish me, you African demon. Burn me in
the fire of your temple, you black god. Let me twist
and turn in your wild and impassioned rites.' Right
here is the source of the fire; here the temple.
Nothing. The sun, the desert, desiccated plants and
emaciated animals. The frame of the lorry shudders
as it descends into a small wadi. We pass by the
bones of a camel that has perished from thirst in
this wilderness. Mustafa Sa'eed's face returns to my

mind's eye in the form of his elder son's face – the one who most resembles him.

On the day of the circumcision Mahjoub and I drank more than we should. Owing to the monotony of their lives the people in our village make of every happy event however small an excuse for holding a sort of wedding party. At night I pulled him by the hand, while the singers sang and the men were clapping deep inside the house. We stood in front of the door of that room. I said to him, 'I alone have the key.' An iron door.

Mahjoub said to me in his inebriated voice: 'Do you know what's inside?'

'Yes,' I said to him.

'What?' he said.

'Nothing,' I said, laughing under the influence of the drink. 'Absolutely nothing. This room is a big joke – like life. You imagine it contains a secret and there's nothing there. Absolutely nothing.'

'You're drunk,' said Mahjoub. 'This room is filled from floor to ceiling with treasures: gold, jewels, pearls. Do you know who Mustafa Sa'eed is?'

I told him that Mustafa Sa'eed was a lie. 'Do you want to know the truth about Mustafa Sa'eed?' I said to him with another drunken laugh.

'You're not only drunk but mad,' said Mahjoub. 'Mustafa Sa'eed is in fact the Prophet El-Kidr, suddenly making his appearance and as suddenly vanishing. The treasures that lie in this room are like those of King Solomon, brought here by genies, and you have the key to that treasure. Open, Sesame, and let's distribute the gold and jewels to the people.' Mahjoub was about to shout out and gather the people together had I not put my hand over his mouth. The next morning each of us woke up in his own house not knowing how he'd got there.

The road is endless, without limit, the sun indefatigable. No wonder Mustafa Sa'eed fled to the bitter cold of the North. Isabella Seymour said to him: 'The Christians say their God was crucified that he might bear the burden of their sins. He died, then, in vain, for what they call sin is nothing but the sigh of contentment in embracing you, O pagan god of mine. You are my god and there is no god but you.' No doubt that was the reason for her suicide, and not that she was ill with cancer. She was a believer when she met him. She denied her religion and worshipped a god like the calf of the Children of Israel. How strange! How ironic! Just because a man has been created on the Equator some mad people regard him as a slave, others as a god. Where lies the mean? Where the middle way? And my grandfather, with his thin voice and that mischievous laugh of his when in a good humour, where is *his* place in the scheme of things? Is he really as I assert and as he appears to be? Is he above this chaos? I don't know. In any case he has survived despite epidemics, the corruption of those in power, and the cruelty of nature. I am certain that when death appears to him he will smile in death's face. Isn't this enough? Is more than this demanded of a son of Adam?

From behind a hill there came into view a bedouin, who hurried towards us, crossing the car's path. We drew up. His body and clothes were the colour of the earth. The driver asked him what he wanted.

He said, 'Give me a cigarette or some tobacco for the sake of Allah – for two days I haven't tasted tobacco.' As we had no tobacco I gave him a cigarette. We thought we might as well stop a while and give ourselves a rest from sitting.

Never in my life have I seen a man smoke a cigarette with such gusto. Squatting down on his backside, the bedouin began gulping in the smoke with indescribable avidity. After a couple of minutes he put out his hand and I gave him another cigarette, which he devoured as he had done the first. Then he began writhing on the ground as though in an epileptic fit, after which he stretched himself out, encircled his head with his hands, and went stiff and lifeless as though dead. All the time we were there, around twenty minutes, he stayed like this, until the engine started up, when he jumped to his feet – a man brought back to life – and began thanking me and asking Allah to grant me long life, so I threw him the packet with the rest of the cigarettes. Dust rose up behind us, and I watched the bedouin running towards some tattered tents by some bushes south-wards of us, where there were diminutive sheep and naked children. Where, O God, is the shade? Such land brings forth nothing but prophets. This drought can be cured only by the sky.

The road is unending and the sun merciless. Now the car lets out a wailing sound as it passes over a stony surface, flat as a table. 'We are a doomed people, so regale us with amusing stories.' Who said this? Then: 'Like someone marooned in the desert who has covered no distance yet spared no mount.' The driver is not talking; he is merely an extension of the machine in his charge, sometimes cursing and swearing at it, while the country around us is a circle sunk in the mirage. 'One mirage kept raising us up, another casting us down, and from deserts we were spewed out into yet more deserts.' Mohamed Sa'eed El-Abbasi, what a poet he was! And Abu Nuwas: 'We drank as deeply as a people athirst since the age of Aad.' This is the land of despair and poetry but there is nobody to sing.

We came across a government car that had broken down, with five soldiers and a sergeant, all armed with rifles, surrounding it. We drew up and they drank from the water we had and ate some of our provisions, and we let them have some petrol. They said that a woman from the tribe of El-Mirisab had killed her husband and the government was in the process of arresting her. What was her name? What his? Why had she killed him? They do not know – only that she is from the El-Mirisab tribe and that she had killed a man who was her husband. But they would know it: the tribes of El-Mirisab, El-Hawaweer and El-Kababeesh; the judges, resident and itinerant; the Commissioner of North Kordofan, the Commissioner of the Southern North Province, the Commissioner of East Khartoum; the shepherds at the watering places; the Sheikhs and the Nazirs; the bedouin in hair tents at the intersections of the valleys. All of them would know her name, for it is not every day that a woman kills a man, let alone her husband, in this land in which the sun has left no more killing to be done. An idea occurred to me; turning it over in my mind, I decided to express it and see what happened. I said to them that she had not killed him but that he had died from sunstroke – just as Isabella Seymour had died, and Sheila Greenwood, Ann Hammond, and Jean Morris. Nothing happened.

'We had a horrible Commandant of Police called Major Cook,' said the sergeant. No use. No sense of wonder. They went on their way and we went on ours.

The sun is the enemy. Now it is exactly in the liver of the sky, as the Arabs say. What a fiery liver! And thus it will remain for hours without moving – or so it will seem to living creatures when even the stones groan, the trees weep, and iron cries out for help. The weeping of a woman under a man at dawn and two wide-open white thighs. They are now like the dry bones of camels scattered in the desert. No taste. No smell. Nothing of good. Nothing of evil. The wheels of the car strike spitefully against the stones. 'His twisted road all too soon leads to disaster, and generally the disaster lies clearly before him, as clear as the sun, so that we are amazed how such an intelligent man can in fact be so stupid. Granted a generous measure of intelligence, he has been denied wisdom. He is an intelligent fool.' That's what the judge said at the Old Bailey before passing sentence.

The road is endless and the sun as bright as it proverbially is. I shall write to Mrs Robinson. She lives in Shanklin on the Isle of Wight. Her address has stuck in my memory ever since Mustafa Sa'eed's conversation that night. Her husband died of typhoid and was buried in Cairo in the cemetery of the Imam Shafi'i. Yes, he embraced Islam. Mustafa

Sa'eed said she attended the trial from beginning to end. He was composed the whole time. After sentence was given he wept on her breast. She stroked his head, kissed him on the forehead, and said, 'Don't cry, dear child.' She had not liked Jean Morris and had warned him against marrying her. I shall write to her; perhaps she can throw some light on things, perhaps she remembers things he forgot or did not mention. And suddenly the war ended in victory. The glow of sundown is not blood but henna on a woman's foot, and the breeze that pursues us from the Nile Valley carries a perfume whose smell will not fade from my mind as long as I live. And just as a caravan of camels makes a halt, so did we. The greater part of the journey was behind us. We ate and drank. Some of us performed the night prayer, while the driver and his assistants took some bottles of drink from the lorry. I threw myself down on the sand, lighted a cigarette and lost myself in the splendour of the sky. The lorry too was nourished with water, petrol and oil, and now there it is, silent and content like a mare in her stable. The war ended in victory for us all: the stones, the trees, the animals, and the iron, while I, lying under this beautiful, compassionate sky, feel that we are all brothers; he who drinks and he who prays and he who steals and he who commits adultery and he who fights and he who kills. The source is the same. No one knows what goes on in the mind of the Divine. Perhaps He doesn't care. Perhaps He is not angry. On a night such as this you feel you are able to rise up to the sky on a rope ladder. This is the land of poetry and the possible – and my daughter is named

Hope. We shall pull down and we shall build, and we shall humble the sun itself to our will; and somehow we shall defeat poverty. The driver, who had kept silent the whole day, has now raised his voice in song: a sweet, rippling voice that you can't imagine is his. He is singing to his car just as the poets of old sang to their camels:

How shapely is your steering-wheel astride its metal stem.
No sleep or rest tonight we'll have till Sitt Nafour is come.

Another voice is raised in answer:

From the lands of Kawal and Kambu on a journey we are bent.
His head he tossed with noble pride, resigned to our intent.
The sweat pours down his mighty neck and soaks his massive sides
And sparks around his feet do fly as to the sands he strides.

Then a third voice rose up in answer to the other two:

Woe to me, what pain does grip my breast
As does the quarry tire my dog in chase.
The man of God his very faith you'd wrest
And turn aside at Jeddah the pilgrim to Hejaz.

And so we continued on, while every vehicle, coming or going, would stop and join us until we became a huge caravanserai of more than a hundred men who ate and drank and prayed and got drunk.

We formed ourselves into a large circle into which some of the younger men entered and danced in the manner of girls. We clapped, stamped on the ground, and hummed in unison, making a festival to nothingness in the heart of the desert. Then someone produced a transistor radio which we placed in the centre of the circle and we clapped and danced to its music. Someone else got the idea of having the drivers line up their cars in a circle and train their headlights on to the ring of dancers so that there was a blaze of light the like of which I do not believe that place had ever seen before. The men imitated the loud trilling cries women utter at festivities and the horns of the cars all rang out together. The light and the clamour attracted the bedouin from the neighbouring wadi ravines and foothills, both men and women, people whom you would not see by day, when it was just as if they melted away under the light of the sun. A vast concourse of people gathered.

Actual women entered the circle; had you seen them by day you would not have given them a second glance, but at that time and place they were beautiful. A bedouin man brought a sheep which he tied up and slaughtered and then roasted over a fire. One of the travellers produced two crates of beer which he distributed around as he called out, 'To the good health of the Sudan. To the good health of the Sudan.' Packets of cigarettes and boxes of sweets were passed round, and the bedouin women sang and danced, the night and the desert resounding with the echoes of a great feast, as though we were some tribe of genies. A feast without a meaning, a mere desperate act that had sprung up impromptu like the small whirlwinds that rise up in the desert and then die. At dawn we parted. The bedouin made their way back to the wadi ravines. The people exchanged shouts of 'Good-bye, good-bye', and everyone ran off to his car. The engines revved up and the headlights veered away from the place which moments before had been an intimate stage and which now returned to its former state – a tract of desert. Some of the headlights pointed southwards in the direction of the Nile, some northwards also in the direction of the Nile. The dust swirled up and disappeared. We caught up the sun on the peaks of the mountains of Kerari overlooking Omdurman.

The steamer swung round on itself so that its engines would not be working against the current. Everything happened as it always did: the raucous whistle and the small boats from the opposite shore, the sycamore trees and the bustle on the quay of the landing-stage. Except for one great difference: I stepped ashore and Mahjoub shook me by the hand, avoiding me with his eyes; this time he was the only one who had come to meet me. He was embarrassed, as though feeling guilty about something or as though he were putting the responsibility on to me.

Hardly had I shaken hands with him than I said, 'How did you let this happen?'

'What has happened has happened,' said Mahjoub, fixing the saddle of the tall black donkey which belonged to my uncle Abdul Karim. 'The two boys are well and are at my place.'

I had not thought of the boys during the whole of that ghastly journey. I had been thinking of her. Again I said to Mahjoub: 'What happened?'

He was still avoiding looking at me. He remained silent, adjusting the sheepskin cover on the saddle and tightening the girth round his donkey's belly. He pushed the saddle slightly forward, seized hold of the reins and jumped on. I remained standing, awaiting the reply that did not come; then I too mounted. Urging the donkey on, he said to me: 'It's as I told you in the cable. There's no point in delving into the matter. In any case we weren't expecting you.'

'I wish I'd done as you advised and married her,' I said to him, encouraging him to speak. All I succeeded in doing, though, was to drive him into a deeper silence. He was clearly angry, for he dug his heel sharply into his donkey, though it had done nothing to deserve such treatment. 'Ever since I got your cable,' I said to him, chasing after him but without quite catching him up, 'I haven't slept or eaten or spoken to a soul. Three days travelling from Khartoum by rail and steamer I've spent thinking and asking myself how it happened and I find no answer.'

'You've never spent such a short time away from the village,' he said kindly, as though feeling sorry for me.

'No,' I said to him. 'Thirty-two days to be exact.'

'Anything new in Khartoum?' he said.

'We were busy with a conference,' I said to him. Interest showed on his face, for he liked to have news of Khartoum, especially news of scandals and stories of bribery and of the corruption of those in power.

'What were they in conference about this time?' he said with evident interest.

I was upset that he should have so quickly forgotten the matter in hand. 'The Ministry of Education,' I said to him wearily, wishing to cut it short, 'organized a conference to which it invited delegates from twenty African countries to discuss ways of unifying educational methods throughout the whole continent – I was a member of the secretariat of the conference.'

'Let them build the schools first,' said Mahjoub, 'and then discuss unifying education. How do these people's minds work? They waste time in conferences and poppycock and here are our children having to travel several miles to school. Aren't we human beings? Don't we pay taxes? Haven't we any rights in this country? Everything's in Khartoum. The whole of the country's budget is spent in Khartoum. One single hospital in Merawi, and it takes us three days to get there. The women die in childbirth – there's not a single qualified midwife in this place. And you, what are you doing in Khartoum? What's the use in our having one of us in the government when you're not doing anything?'

My donkey had passed him, so I pulled at the reins till he caught up with me. I chose to keep silent, although if it had been any other time I would have shouted at him – he and I had been like that since childhood, shouting at each other when angry, then making it up and forgetting. But now I was hungry and tired and my heart was heavy with grief. Had the circumstances of our meeting this time been better I would have roused him to laughter and to anger with stories about that conference. He will not believe the facts about the new rulers of Africa, smooth of face, lupine of mouth, their hands gleaming with rings of precious stones, exuding perfume from their cheeks, in white, blue, black and green suits of fine mohair and expensive silk rippling on their shoulders like the fur of Siamese cats, and with shoes that reflect the light from chandeliers and squeak as they tread on marble. Mahjoub will not believe that for nine days they studied every aspect of the progress of education in Africa in the Independence Hall built for the purpose and costing more than a million pounds: an imposing edifice of stone, cement, marble and glass, constructed in the form of a complete circle and designed in London, its corridors of white marble brought from Italy and the windows made up of small pieces of coloured glass skilfully arranged in a framework of teak. The floor of the main hall was covered with fine Persian carpets, while the ceiling was in the form of a gilded dome; on all sides chandeliers hung down, each the size of a large camel. The platform on which the Ministers of Education in Africa took it in turns to stand for nine whole days was of red marble like that of Napoleon's tomb at Les Invalides, its vast ebony surface smooth and shiny. On the walls were oil paintings, and facing the main entrance was a vast map of Africa fashioned in coloured mosaic, each country in a different colour. How can I say to Mahjoub that the Minister who said in his verbose address, received with a storm of clapping: 'No contradiction must occur between what the student learns at school and between the reality of the life of the people. Everyone who is educated today wants to sit at a comfortable desk under a fan and live in an air-conditioned house surrounded by a garden, coming and going in an American car as wide as the street. If we do not tear out this disease by the roots we shall have with us a bourgeoisie that is in no way connected with the reality of our life, which is more dangerous to the future of Africa than imperialism itself': how can I say to Mahjoub that this very man escapes during the summer months from Africa to his villa on Lake Lucerne and that his wife does her shopping at Harrods in London, from where the articles are flown to her in a private plane, and that the members of his delegation themselves openly say that he is corrupt and takes bribes, that he has acquired whole estates, has set up businesses and amassed properties, has created a vast fortune from the sweat dripping from the brows of wretched, half-naked people in the jungle? Such people are concerned only with their stomachs and their sensual pleasures. There is no justice or moderation in the world Mustafa Sa'eed said: 'But I seek not glory, for the likes of me do not seek glory.' Had he returned in the natural way of things he would have joined up with this pack of wolves. They all resemble him: handsome faces and faces made so by comfortable living. One of those Ministers said in the closing party of the conference that Mustafa had been his teacher. The first thing he did when they introduced me to him was to exclaim: 'You remind me of a dear friend with whom I was on very close terms in London – Dr Mustafa Sa'eed. He used to be my teacher. In 1928 he was President of the Society for the Struggle for African Freedom of which I was a committee member. What a man he was! He's one of the greatest Africans I've known. He had wide contacts. Heavens, that man – women fell for him like flies. He used to say "I'll liberate Africa with my penis", and he laughed so widely you could see the back of his throat.' I wanted to put some questions to him but he disappeared in the throng of Presidents and Ministers. Mustafa no longer concerns me, for Mahjoub's telegram has changed everything, bringing me worries of my own. When I first read Mrs Robinson's reply to my letter I had a feeling of immense joy. I read it in the train a second time and tried, though in vain, to banish my thoughts from the spot that had become the pivot round which they revolved.

The donkeys continued to toss up the stones with their hooves. 'Why so silent, as though you've lost your tongue? Why don't you say something?' said Mahjoub.

'Civil servants like me can't change anything,' I said to him.

'If our masters say "Do so-and-so", we do it. You're the head of the National Democratic Socialist Party here. It's the party in power, so why not pour out your anger on them?'

Mahjoub said apologetically, 'If it hadn't been for this . . . this calamity . . . On the day it happened we were preparing to travel in a delegation to ask for the building of a large hospital, also for an intermediate boys' school, a primary school for girls, an agricultural school and . . .' Suddenly he broke off and retired into his angry silence.

I glanced at the river on our left gleaming with menace and reverberating with mysterious sound. Then, in front of us, there came into view the ten domes in the middle of the cemetery, and the recollection it called forth cut into my heart.

'We buried them without any fuss, first thing in

the morning,' said Mahjoub. 'We told the women not to mourn. We held no funeral ceremony and informed no one – the police would only have come along and there would have been all the scandal of an investigation.'

'Why the police?' I asked in alarm.

He looked at me for a while, then fell silent. A long time later he said: 'A week or ten days after you went away her father said he had given Wad Rayyes a promise – and they married her off to him. Her father swore at her and beat her; he told her she'd marry him whether she liked it or not. I didn't attend the marriage ceremony; no one was there except his friends: Bakri, your grandfather, and Bint Mahjoub. For myself, I tried to deflect Wad Rayyes from his purpose, but like someone obsessed he insisted. I talked to her father, who said he wouldn't be made a laughing-stock by people saying his daughter wouldn't listen to him. After the marriage I told Wad Rayyes to go about things with tact. For two weeks they remained together without exchanging a word. She was – he was in an indescribable state, like a madman. He complained to all and sundry, saying how could there be in his house a woman he'd married according to the laws of God and His Prophet and how could there not be between them the normal relationship of man and wife. We used to tell him to have patience, then . . .'

The two donkeys suddenly brayed at the same time and I almost fell out of the saddle. For two whole days I went on asking people about it, but no one would tell me. They all avoided looking at me as though they were accomplices in some dire crime.

'Why did you leave your work and con
mother said to me.

'The two boys,' I said to her.

She looked at me searchingly for a while and said:
'The boys or the boys' mother? What was there
between you and her? She came to your father and
her very words to him were: "Tell him to marry
me!" What an impudent hussy! That's modern
women for you! That was bad enough, but the
terrible thing she did later was even worse.'

My grandfather too vouchsafed me no informa-
tion. I found him seated on his couch in a state of
fatigue I'd never seen him in before, just as if the
source of life inside him had suddenly dried up.
I sat on and he still did not speak, only sighed from
time to time and fidgeted and called upon God to
grant him refuge from the accursed Devil. Every
time he did this I would feel twinges of conscience
as though the Devil and I were in some sort of
league together. After a long time, addressing the
ceiling, he said: 'God curse all women! Women are
the sisters of the Devil. Wad Rayyes! Wad Rayyes!'
and my grandfather burst into tears. It was the first
time in my life I had seen him crying. He cried much,
then wiped away the tears with the hem of his robe
and was so long silent that I thought he had gone to
sleep. 'God rest your soul, Wad Rayyes,' he said after
a while. 'May God forgive him and encompass him
with His mercy.' He muttered some prayers and
said: 'He was a man without equal – always laughing, always at hand when one was in trouble. He
never said "No" to anyone who asked anything of
him. If only he'd listened to me! To end up like that!

There is no power and no strength save in God – it's the first time anything like this has happened in the village since God created it. What a time of affliction we live in!'

'What happened?' I asked him, plucking up courage.

He took no notice of my question and became engrossed in his string of prayer-beads. Then he said: 'Nothing but trouble comes from that tribe. I said to Wad Rayyes, "This woman's a bringer of bad luck. Keep away from her." However, it was fated.'

On the morning of the third day, with a bottle of whisky in my pocket, I went off to see Bint Majzoub. If Bint Majzoub would not tell me, then no one would. Bint Majzoub, pouring some whisky into a large aluminium cup, said: 'No doubt you want something. We're not used to having such fine city drink here.'

'I wish to know what happened,' I said to her. 'No one wants to tell me.'

She took a large gulp from the cup, gave a scowl, and said: 'The thing done by Bint Mahmoud is not easily spoken of. It is something we have never seen or heard of in times past or present.'

She stopped talking and I waited patiently till a third of the bottle had gone, without it having any effect on her except that she looked more animated.

'That's enough of the heathens' drink,' said Bint Majzoub, closing the bottle. 'It's certainly formidable stuff and not a bit like date arak.'

I looked at her pleadingly. 'The things I'm going to say to you,' she said, 'you won't hear from a living soul in the village – they buried them with Bint Mahmoud and with poor Wad Rayyes. They are shameful things and it's hard to talk about them.' Then she gave me a searching look with her bold eyes.

'These are words that won't please you,' she said, 'especially if . . .' and she lowered her head for an instant.

'Just like everyone else,' I said, 'I want to know what happened. Why should I be the only one who mustn't be allowed to know?'

She drew on the cigarette I gave her. 'Some time after the evening prayer,' she continued, 'I awoke to the screaming of Hosna Bint Mahmoud in Wad Rayyes's house. The whole village was silent, you couldn't hear a sound. To tell you God's truth, I thought that Wad Rayyes had at last achieved what he wanted – the poor man was on the verge of madness: two weeks with the woman without her speaking to him or allowing him to come near her. I gave ear for a time as she screamed and wailed. May God forgive me, I laughed as I heard her screaming, telling myself that Wad Rayyes still had something left in him. The screaming grew louder and I heard a movement in Bakri's house alongside Wad Rayyes's. I heard Bakri shouting, "You should be ashamed of yourself, man, making such a scandal and hullabaloo." Then I heard the voice of Sa'eeda, Bakri's wife, saying, "Bint Mahmoud, look to your honour. What scandals are these? A virgin bride doesn't behave like this – as though you'd had no experience of men." Bint Mahmoud's screams grew louder. Then I heard Wad Rayyes screaming at the top of his voice, "Bakri! Hajj Ahmed! Bint Majzoub! Help! Bint Mahmoud has killed me." I leapt up from bed and rushed out in a state of undress. I rapped on Bakri's door and on Mahjoub's, then ran to Wad Rayyes's, which I found closed. I cried out at the top of my voice, at which Mahjoub came along, then Bakri. Many people then gathered round us. As we were breaking down the courtyard door we heard a scream – a mountain-shattering scream from Wad Rayyes, then a similar scream from Bint Mahmoud. We entered, Mahjoub, Bakri and I. "Stop the people from entering the house," I said to Mahjoub. "Don't let any woman enter the house." Mahjoub went out and shouted at the people; when he returned your uncle Abdul Karim was with him, also Sa'eed, Tahir Rawwasi, and even your poor grandfather came from his house.'

The sweat began pouring down Bint Majzoub's face. Her throat was dry and she pointed to the water. When I had brought it to her she drank, wiped the sweat from her face, and said, 'I ask pardon and repentance of Almighty God. We found the two of them in Wad Rayyes's low-ceilinged room looking on to the street. The lamp was alight. Wad Rayyes was as naked as the day he was born; Bint Mahmoud too was naked apart from her torn underclothes. The red straw mat was swimming in blood. I raised the lamp and saw that every inch of Bint Mahmoud's body was covered in bites and scratches – her stomach, thighs and neck. The nipple of one breast had been bitten through and blood poured down from her lower lip. There is no strength and no power save in God. Wad Rayyes had been stabbed more than ten times – in his stomach, chest, face, and between his thighs.'

Bint Majzoub was unable to continue. She swallowed with difficulty and her throat quivered nervously. Then she said: 'O Lord, there is no opposition to Thy will. We found her lying on her back with the knife plunged into her heart. Her mouth was open and her eyes were staring as though she were alive. Wad Rayyes had his tongue lolling out from between his jaws and his arms were raised in the air.'

Bint Majzoub covered her face with her hand and the sweat trickled down between her fingers; her breathing was fast and laboured. 'I ask forgiveness of Almighty God,' she said with difficulty. 'They had both died minutes beforehand. The blood was still warm and dripped from Bint Mahmoud's heart and from between Wad Rayyes's thighs. Blood covered the mat and the bed and flowed in rivulets across the floor of the room. Mahjoub, God lengthen his life, was a tower of strength. When he heard Mahmoud's voice he hurried outside and told your father not to let him in. Then Mahjoub and the men bore off Wad Rayyes's body, while Bakri's wife and I, with some of the older women, took care of Bint Mahmoud. We put them in their shrouds that very night and they took them away before sunrise and buried them – she beside her mother and he beside his first wife, Bint Rajab. Some of the women started to hold a funeral ceremony but Mahjoub, God bless him, shut them up and said he'd break the neck of anyone who opened her mouth. What sort of funeral ceremony, my child, can be held in such circumstances? This is a great catastrophe that has befallen the village. All our lives we have enjoyed God's protection and now finally something like this happens to us! I ask forgiveness and repentance of Thee, O Lord.'

She too wept as my grandfather had done. She wept long and bitterly; then, smiling through her tears, she said, 'The strange thing about it is that his eldest wife Mabrouka didn't wake up at all, despite all the shouting that brought people right from the far end of the village. When I went to her and shook her, she raised her head and said, "Bint Majzoub, what's brought you at this hour?" "Get up," I said to her. "There's been a murder in your house." "Whose murder?" she said. "Bint Mahmoud has killed Wad Rayyes and then killed herself," I said to her. "Good riddance!" she said and went back to sleep, and we could hear her snoring while we were busy preparing Bint Mahmoud for burial. When the people returned from the burial, we found Mabrouka sitting drinking her morning coffee. When some of the women wanted to commiserate with her she yelled, "Women, let everyone of you go about her business. Wad Rayyes dug his grave with his own hands, and Bint Mahmoud, God's blessings be upon her, paid him out in full." Then she gave trilling cries of joy. Yes, by God, my child, she gave trilling cries of joy and said to the women,

"It's too bad, but if anyone doesn't like it she can go drink river water." I ask forgiveness of Almighty God. Her father, Mahmoud, almost killed himself with weeping that night – he was bellowing like an ox. Your grandfather was cursing and swearing, laying about him with his stick, yelling and weeping. For no reason your uncle Abdul Karim quarrelled with Bakri. "A murder happens next door to you," he said to him, "and you sleep right through it?" It was the same thing with the whole village that night – it was as though they'd been visited by devils. Mahjoub alone was calm and collected and saw to everything: he brought shrouds from we don't know where, and he quietened down Wad Rayyes's boys who were making a terrible noise. May God spare you such a sight, my child – it was something to break one's heart and bring white hair to a baby's head. And it was all without rhyme or reason. She accepted the stranger – why didn't she accept Wad Rayyes?'

The fields are all fire and smoke. It is the time for preparing to sow the wheat. They clean the ground and collect up the sticks of maize and small stems, mementos of the season that has ended, and make them into burning heaps. The earth is black and level, ready for the coming event. The men's bodies are bent over their hoes; some are walking behind the ploughs. The tops of the palm trees shudder in the gentle breeze and grow still. Under the sun's violence at midday hot steam rises from the fields of watered clover. Every breath of wind diffuses the scent of lemon, orange and tangerine. The lowing of an ox, the braying of a donkey, or the sound of an axe on wood. Yet the world has changed.

I found Mahjoub mud-bespattered, his body naked except for the rag round his middle, moist with sweat, trying to separate a shoot from the mother date palm. I did not greet him and he did not turn to me but went on digging round the shoot. I remained standing, watching him. Then I lit a cigarette and held out the packet to him, but he refused with a shake of his head. I took my cares off to the trunk of a nearby date palm against which I rested my head. There is no room for me here. Why don't I pack up and go? Nothing astonishes these people. They take everything in their stride. They neither rejoice at a birth nor are saddened at a death. When they laugh they say 'I ask forgiveness of God' and when they weep they say 'I ask forgiveness of God.' Just that. And I, what have I learnt? They have learnt silence and patience from the river and from the trees. And I, what have I learnt? I noticed that Mahjoub was biting his lower lip as was his habit when engaged on some job of work. I used to beat him in wrestling and running, but he would outstrip me in swimming the river to the other bank and in climbing palm trees. No palm tree was too difficult for him. There was between us the sort of affection that exists between blood brothers. Mahjoub swore at the small palm tree when he eventually succeeded in separating it from the trunk of its mother without breaking its roots. He heaped earth on to the large wound that was left in the trunk, lopped the stalks from the small plant and removed the earth, then threw it down to dry out in the sun. I told myself that he would now be more prepared to talk. He came into the shade where I was, sat down and stretched out his legs. He remained silent for a while, then sighed and said, 'I ask forgiveness of God.' He stretched out his hand and I gave him a cigarette – he only smoked when I was at the village and would say, 'we're burning the government's money.'

He threw away the cigarette before finishing it. 'You look ill,' he said. 'The journey must have tired you out. Your presence wasn't necessary. When I sent you the telegram I didn't expect you'd come.'

'She killed him and killed herself,' I said as though talking to myself. 'She stabbed him more than ten times and – how ghastly!'

'Who told you?' he said, turning to me in astonishment.

'He bit off her nipple,' I continued, giving no heed to his questions, 'and bit and scratched every inch of her body. How ghastly!'

'It must have been Bint Majzoub who told you,' he shouted angrily. 'God curse her, she can't hold her tongue. These are things that shouldn't be spoken about.'

'Whether they're spoken about or not,' I said to him, 'they've happened. They happened in front of your very eyes and you did nothing. You, you're a leader in the village and you did nothing.'

'What should we do?' said Mahjoub. 'Why didn't

you do something? Why didn't you marry her? You're only any good when it comes to talking. It was the woman herself who had the impudence to speak her mind. We've lived in an age when we've seen women wooing men.'

'And what did she say?' I said to him.

'It's over and done with,' he said. 'What's the use of talking? Give thanks to God that you didn't marry her. The thing she did wasn't the act of a human being – it was the act of a devil.'

'What did she say?' I said to him, grinding my teeth.

'When her father went and swore at her,' he said, looking at me without sympathy, 'she came to my home at sunrise. She said she wanted you to save her from Wad Rayyes and the attention of suitors. All she wanted was to become formally married to you, nothing more. She said, "He'll leave me with my children and I want nothing whatsoever from him." I told her we shouldn't involve you in the matter, and I advised her to accept the situation. Her father had charge of her and was free to act as he thought fit. I told her Wad Rayyes wouldn't live for ever. A mad man and a mad woman – how can we be to blame? What could we do about it? Her poor father has been confined to bed ever since that ill-fated day; he never goes out, never meets anyone. What can I or anyone else do if the world's gone crazy. Bint Mahmoud's madness was of a kind never seen before.'

I had to make a great effort not to break into tears. 'Hosna wasn't mad,' I said. 'She was the sanest woman in the village – it's you who're mad. She was the sanest woman in the village – and the most beautiful. Hosna wasn't mad.'

Mahjoub laughed, guffawed with laughter. 'How extraordinary!' I heard him say amidst laughter. 'Take a pull at yourself, man! Wake up! Fancy you falling in love at your age! You've become as mad as Wad Rayyes. Schooling and education have made you soft. You're crying like a woman. Good God, wonders never cease – love, illness and tears, and she wasn't worth a millième. If it wasn't for the sake of decency she wouldn't have been worth burying – we'd have thrown her into the river or left her body out for the hawks.'

I'm not altogether clear as to what happened next. However, I do remember my hands closing over Mahjoub's throat; I remember the way his eyes bulged; I remember, too, a violent blow in the stomach and Mahjoub crouching on my chest. I remember Mahjoub prostrate on the ground and me kicking him, and I remember his voice screaming out 'Mad! You're mad!' I remember a clamour and a shouting as I pressed down on Mahjoub's throat and heard a gurgling sound; then I felt a powerful hand pulling me by the neck and the impact of a heavy stick on my head.

The world has turned suddenly upside down. Love? Love does not do this. This is hatred. I feel hatred and seek revenge; my adversary is within and I needs must confront him. Even so, there is still in my mind a modicum of sense that is aware of the irony of the situation. I begin from where Mustafa Sa'eed had left off. Yet he at least made a choice, while I have chosen nothing. For a while the disk of the sun remained motionless just above the western horizon, then hurriedly disappeared. The armies of darkness, ever encamped near by, bounded in and occupied the world in an instant. If only I had told her the truth perhaps she would not have acted as she did. I had lost the war because I did not know and did not choose. For a long time I stood in front of the iron door. Now I am on my own: there is no escape, no place of refuge, no safeguard. Outside, my world was a wide one; now it had contracted, had withdrawn upon itself, until I myself had become the world, no world existing outside of me. Where, then, were the roots that struck down into times past? Where the memories of death and life? What had happened to the caravan and to the tribe? Where had gone the trilling cries of the women at tens of weddings, where the Nile floodings, and the blowing of the wind summer and winter from north and south? Love? Love does not do this. This is hatred. Here I am, standing in Mustafa Sa'eed's house in front of the iron door, the door of the rectangular room with the triangular roof and the green windows, the key in my pocket and my adversary inside with, doubtless, a fiendish look of happiness on his face. I am the guardian, the lover, and the adversary.

I turned the key in the door, which opened without difficulty. I was met by dampness and an odour like that of an old memory. I know this smell: the smell of sandalwood and incense. I felt my way with my finger-tips along the walls and came up against a window pane. I threw open the window and the wooden shutters. I opened a second window and a third, but all that came in from outside was more darkness. I struck a match. The light exploded on my eyes and out of the darkness there emerged a frowning face with pursed lips that I knew but could not place. I moved towards it with hate in my heart. It was my adversary Mustafa Sa'eed. The face grew a neck, the neck two shoulders and a chest, then a trunk and two legs, and I found myself standing face to face with myself. This is not Mustafa Sa'eed – it's a picture of me frowning at my face from a mirror. Suddenly the picture disappeared and I sat in the darkness for I know not how long listening intently and hearing nothing. I lit another match and a woman gave a bitter smile. Standing in an oasis of light, I looked around me and saw there was an old lamp on the table my hand was almost touching. I shook it and found there was oil in it. How extraordinary! I lit the lamp and the shadows and the walls moved away and the ceiling rose up. I lit the lamp and closed the windows. The smell must remain imprisoned here: the smell of bricks and wood and burning incense and sandalwood – and books. Good God, the four walls from floor to ceiling were filled, shelf upon shelf, with books and more books and yet more books. I lit a cigarette and filled my lungs with the strange smell. What a fool he was! Was this the action of a man who wanted to turn over a new leaf? I shall bring the whole place down upon his head; I shall set it on fire. I set light to the fine rug beneath my feet and for a while watched it devour a Persian king, mounted on a steed, aiming his lance at a fleeing gazelle. I raised the lamp and found that the whole floor of the room was covered with Persian rugs. I saw that the wall opposite the door ended in an empty space. Lamp in hand, I went up to it. How ridiculous! A fireplace – imagine it! A real English fireplace with all the bits and pieces, above it a brass cowl and in front of it a quadrangular area tiled in green marble, with the mantelpiece of blue marble; on either side of the fireplace were two Victorian chairs covered in a figured silk material, while between them stood a round table with books and notebooks on it. I saw the face of the woman who had smiled at me moments before – a large oil portrait in a gilt frame over the mantelpiece; it was signed in the right-hand corner 'M. Sa'eed'. I observed that the fire in the middle of the room was spreading. I took eighteen strides towards it (I counted them as I walked) and trod it out. Though I sought revenge, yet I could not resist my curiosity. First of all I shall see and hear, then I shall burn it down as though it had never been. The books – I could see in the light of the lamp that they were arranged in categories. Books on economics, history and literature. Zoology. Geology. Mathematics. Astronomy. The Encyclopaedia Britannica. Gibbon. Macaulay. Toynbee. The complete works of Bernard Shaw. Keynes. Tawney. Smith. Robinson. *The Economics of Imperfect Competition*. Hobson *Imperialism*. Robinson *An Essay on Marxian Economics*. Sociology. Anthropology. Psychology. Thomas Hardy. Thomas Mann. E. G. Moore. Thomas Moore. Virginia Woolf. Wittgenstein. Einstein. Brierly. Namier. Books I had heard of and others I had not. Volumes of poetry by poets of whom I did not know the existence. *The Journals of Gordon*. *Gulliver's Travels*. Kipling. Housman. *The History of the French Revolution* Thomas Carlyle. *Lectures on the French Revolution* Lord Acton. Books bound in leather. Books in paper covers. Old tattered books. Books that looked as if they'd just come straight from the printers. Huge volumes the size of tombstones. Small books with gilt edges the size of packs of playing cards. Signatures. Words of dedication. Books in boxes. Books on the chairs. Books on the floor. What play-acting is this? What does he mean? Owen. Ford Madox Ford. Stefan Zweig. E. G. Browne. Laski. Hazlitt. *Alice in Wonderland*. Richards. *The Koran* in English. *The Bible* in English. Gilbert Murray. Plato. *The Economics of Colonialism* Mustafa Sa'eed. *Colonialism and Monopoly* Mustafa Sa'eed. *The Cross and Gunpowder* Mustafa Sa'eed. *The Rape of Africa* Mustafa Sa'eed. *Prospero and Caliban*. *Totem and Taboo*. Doughty. Not a single Arabic book. A graveyard. A mausoleum. An insane idea.

A prison. A huge joke. A treasure chamber. 'Open, Sesame, and let's divide up the jewels among the people.' The ceiling was of oak and in the middle was an archway, supported by two marble columns of a yellowish red colour, dividing the room in two; the archway was covered by a faience with decorated edges. I was standing at the head of a long dining-table; I don't know what wood it was made of but its surface was dark and glistening and along two sides were five leather-upholstered chairs. On the right was a settee covered in blue velvet, with cushions of – I touched them: of swansdown. On both sides of the fireplace I saw various objects I had not noticed before: on the right was a long table on which was a silver candelabrum holding ten virgin candles; on the left was another. I lit them candle by candle, and the first thing they cast their light upon was the oil painting above the mantelpiece: the elongated face of a woman with wide eyes and brows that joined above them. The nose was a shade too large and the mouth tended to be too wide. I realized that the glass-fronted bookshelves on the wall opposite the door did not reach to the ground and ended at the two sides of the fireplace with white-painted cupboards that projected two or three feet from the book-shelves. It was the same along the left-hand side. I went up to the photographs ranged on the shelf: Mustafa Sa'eed laughing; Mustafa Sa'eed writing; Mustafa Sa'eed swimming; Mustafa Sa'eed some-where in the country; Mustafa Sa'eed in gown and mortar-board; Mustafa Sa'eed rowing on the Serpentine; Mustafa Sa'eed in a Nativity play, a crown on his head, as one of the Three Kings who brought perfumes and myrrh to Christ; Mustafa Sa'eed standing between a man and a woman. Mustafa Sa'eed had not let a moment pass without recording it for posterity. I took up the picture of a woman and scrutinized it, reading the dedication written in a flowery hand. 'From Sheila with all my love.' Sheila Greenwood no doubt. A country girl from the outskirts of Hull. He had seduced her with presents, honeyed words, and an unfaltering way of seeing things as they really are. The smell of burning sandalwood and incense made her dizzy. She really did have a pretty face. Smiling in the picture, she was wearing a necklace, no doubt an ivory one; her arms were bare and her bosom well-developed. She used to work as a waitress by day and pursue her studies in the evening at the Polytechnic. She was intelligent and believed that the future lay with the working class, that a day would come when class differences would be non-existent and all people would be brothers. 'My mother,' she used to tell him, 'would go mad and my father would kill me if they knew I was in love with a black man, but I don't care.' 'She used to sing me the songs of Marie Lloyd as we lay naked,' he said. 'I would spend Thursday evenings with her in her room in Camden Town and sometimes she would spend the night with me in my flat. She would lick my face with her tongue and say "Your tongue's as crimson as a tropic sunset." I never had enough of her nor she of me. Each time she would gaze at me as though discovering something new. "How marvellous your black colour is!" she would say to me – "the colour of magic and mystery and obscenities."' She committed suicide. Why did Sheila Greenwood commit suicide, Mr Mustafa Sa'eed? I know that you are hiding away somewhere in this Pharaonic tomb which I shall burn over your head. Why did Hosna Bint Mahmoud kill the old man Wad Rayyes and then kill herself in this village in which no one ever kills anyone?

I picked up another photograph and read the dedication which was in a bold, forward-slanting hand: 'To you until death, Isabella.' Poor Isabella Seymour. I feel a special sympathy for Isabella Seymour. Round of face and inclined to plumpness, she wore a dress which was too short for the fashions of those days. She was not, as he had described her, exactly a bronze statue, but there was manifest good nature in her face and an optimistic outlook on life. She smiles. She too is smiling. He said she was the wife of a successful surgeon, the mother of two daughters and a son. She had had eleven years of happy married life, regularly going to church every Sunday morning and participating in charitable organizations. Then she met him and discovered deep within herself dark areas that had previously been closed. Despite everything she left him a letter in which she said, 'If there is a God in Heaven I am sure He will look with sympathetic eye upon the rashness of a poor woman who could not prevent happiness from entering her heart, even if it meant a violation of convention and the wounding of a husband's pride. May God forgive me and may He grant you as much happiness as you have granted me.' I heard his voice on that night, darkly rising and falling, holding neither sadness nor regret; if the voice contained any emotion, then it was a ring of joy. 'I heard her saying to me in an imploring voice of surrender "I love you", and there answered her voice a weak cry from the depths of my consciousness calling on me to desist. But the summit was only a step away, after which I would recover my breath and rest. At the climax of our pain there passed through my head clouds of old, far-off memories, like a vapour rising up from a salt lake in the midst of the desert. When her husband took the stand as a witness in the court, all eyes were on him. He was a man of noble features and gait; his grey head had dignity, while his whole bearing commanded respect. He was a man who, placed against me in the scales, would outweigh me many times over. He was a witness for the defence, not the prosecution. "Fairness demands", he said to the court, over which reigned utter silence, "that I say that my wife Isabella knew she had cancer. In the final period before her death she used to suffer from severe attacks of depression. Several days before her death she confessed to me her relationship with the accused. She said she had fallen in love with him and that there was nothing she could do about it. All through her life with me she had been the model of a true and faithful wife. In spite of everything I feel no bitterness within myself, neither against her nor against the accused. I merely feel a deep sadness at losing her."'

There is no justice or moderation in the world. I feel bitterness and hatred, for after all those victims he crowned his life with yet another one, Hosna Bint Mahmoud, the only woman I have ever loved.

She killed poor Wad Rayyes and killed herself because of Mustafa Sa'eed. I picked up a photograph in a leather frame. This was clearly Ann Hammond, despite the fact she was wearing an Arab robe and head-dress. The dedication under the picture was in shaky Arabic writing: 'From your slave girl, Sausan.' It was a lively face exuding such exuberant good health that the picture could hardly contain it. There was a dimple in each cheek and the lips were full and relaxed; the eyes glowed with curiosity. All this was apparent in the picture despite the years that must have passed since it was taken. 'Unlike me, she yearned for tropical climes, cruel suns, purple horizons. In her eyes I was a symbol of all these hankerings of hers. I am South that yearns for the North and the ice. She owned a flat in Hampstead overlooking the Heath which she would go to from Oxford at week-ends. We would spend Saturday night at my place and Sunday night at hers – and sometimes she would stay on over Monday, sometimes for the whole week. Then she began absenting herself from the University for a month at a time, then two, until she was sent down. She used to bury her face under my armpit and breathe me into herself, as though inhaling some narcotic smoke. Her face would be puckered with pleasure. "I love your sweat," she would say as though intoning rites in a temple. "I want to have the smell of you in full – the smell of rotting leaves in the jungles of Africa, the smell of the mango and the pawpaw and tropical spices, the smell of rains in the deserts of Arabia." She was an easy prey. I had met her following a lecture I gave in Oxford on Abu Nuwas.

I told them that Omar Khayyam was nothing in comparison with Abu Nuwas. I read them some of his poetry about wine in a comic oratorical style which I claimed was how Arabic poetry used to be recited in the Abbasid era. In the lecture I said that Abu Nuwas was a Sufi mystic and that he had made of wine a symbol with which to express all his spiritual yearnings, that the longing for wine in his poetry was really a longing for self-obliteration in the Divine – all arrant nonsense with no basis of fact. However, I was inspired that evening and found the lies tripping off my tongue like sublime truths. Feeling that my elation was communicating itself to my audience, I lied more and more extravagantly. After the lecture they all crowded round me: retired civil servants who had worked in the East, old women whose husbands had died in Egypt, Iraq and the Sudan, men who had fought with Kitchener and Allenby, orientalists, and officials in the Colonial Office and the Middle East section of the Foreign Office. Suddenly I saw a girl of eighteen or nineteen rushing towards me through the ranks of people. She put her arms around me and kissed me. "You are beautiful beyond description," she said, speaking in Arabic, "and the love I have for you is beyond description." With an emotion the violence of which frightened me, I said: "At last I have found you, Sausan. I searched everywhere for you and was afraid I would never find you. Do you remember?" "How can I forget our house in Karkh in Baghdad on the banks of the river Tigris in the days of El-Ma' moun," she said with an emotion no less intense than mine. "I too have followed your footsteps across the centuries, but I was certain we would find each other – and here you are, my darling Mustafa, unchanged since we parted." It was as if she and I were on a stage surrounded by actors who were performing minor roles. I was the hero and she the heroine. The lights went down, darkness reigned all round us, and she and I remained alone in the middle of the stage with a single light trained upon us. Though I realized I was lying, I felt that some-how I meant what I was saying and that she too, despite her lying, was telling the truth. It was one of those rare moments of ecstasy for which I would sell my whole life; a moment in which, before your very eyes, lies are turned into truths, history becomes a pimp, and the jester is turned into a sultan. Still in the exuberance of that dream, she took me to London in her car. She drove with terrifying speed and from time to time would let go of the driving-wheel and put her arms round me. "How happy I am to have found you at last!" she shouted. "I'm so happy I wouldn't care if I died this very instant." We stopped at pubs on the way, sometimes drinking cider, sometimes beer, red wine, white wine, and sometimes we drank whisky, and with every glass I would quote to her from the poetry of Abu Nuwas. I quoted:

> "*Does it not please you the earth is awaking,*
> *That old virgin wine is there for the taking?*
> *Let's have no excuse, come enjoy this delight;*
> *Its mother is green, its sire black as night.*
> *Make haste, Karkh's gardens hang heavy with bloom,*
> *Safe and unscathed from War's blighting doom.*"

'I also quoted to her the lines:

"Full many a glass clear as the lamp of Heaven did I drink
Over a kiss or in promise of a tryst we'd keep;
So matured it was by time that you would think
Beams of light out of the sky did seep."

'Then I quoted:

"When the man of war his knights for war deploys,
And Death's banner calls alike to grey-beards and to boys,
When fires of destruction rage and battle starts,
We, using our hands as bows, with lilies as our darts,
Turn war to revelry and still the best of friends we stay.
When on their drums they beat, we on our lutes do play
To young men who death in pleasure count a sacrifice divine,
While fair cup-bearer, subject of our strife, restores to us the plundered wine,
So insistent he, scarce a glass goes empty than it's filled again.
Here a man reels drunkenly, there another by excess is slain.
This is true war, not a war that between man and man brings strife;
In it with wine we kill and our dead with wine we bring to life."

'And so it was with us: she, moved by poetry and drink, feeding me with sweet lies, while I wove for her intricate and terrifying threads of fantasy. She would tell me that in my eyes she saw the shimmer of mirages in hot deserts, that in my voice she heard the screams of ferocious beasts in the jungles. And I would tell her that in the blueness of her eyes I saw the faraway shoreless seas of the North. In London I took her to my house, the den of lethal lies that I had deliberately built up, lie upon lie: the sandalwood and incense; the ostrich feathers and ivory and ebony figurines; the paintings and drawings of forests of palm trees along the shores of the Nile, boats with sails like doves' wings, suns setting over the mountains of the Red Sea, camel caravans wending their way along sand dunes on the borders of the Yemen, boabab trees in Kordofan, naked girls from the tribes of the Zandi, the Nuer and the Shuluk, fields of banana and coffee on the Equator, old temples in the district of Nubia; Arabic books with decorated covers written in ornate Kufic script; Persian carpets, pink curtains, large mirrors on the walls, and coloured lights in the corners. She knelt and kissed my feet. "You are Mustafa, my master and my lord," she said, "and I am Sausan, your slave girl." And so, in silence, each one of us chose his role, she to act the part of the slave girl and I that of the master. She prepared the bath, then washed me with water in which she had poured essence of roses. She lit the joss-sticks and the sandalwood in the Maghrabi brass brazier hanging in the entrance. She put on an aba and head-dress, while I stretched out on the bed and she massaged my chest, legs, neck and shoulders. "Come here," I said to her imperiously. "To hear is to obey, O master!" she answered me in a subdued voice. While still in the throes of fantasy, intoxication and madness, I took her and she accepted, for what happened had already happened between us a thousand years ago. They found her dead in her flat in Hampstead, having gassed herself:

they also found a note saying: "Mr Sa'eed, God damn you!"'

I put back Ann Hammond's picture in its place to the left of the photograph of Mustafa Sa'eed standing between Mrs Robinson and her husband, on which the dedication at the bottom read, 'To dear Moozie – Cairo 17/4/1913'. It seems that she used to use 'Moozie' as a pet name, for in her letter she also refers to him by it. Mustafa Sa'eed, though frowning, looks a mere child in the picture. Mrs Robinson stands to his left, her arm round his shoulders, while her husband's arm embraces the two of them, and both he and his wife are smiling naturally and happily; their faces are those of young people who have not yet reached their thirties. Despite everything, Mrs Robinson's love for him did not waver. She attended the trial from beginning to end and heard every word, yet in her letter to me she said:

'I cannot express the extent of my gratitude to you for having written to me about dear Moozie. Moozie was, for my husband and me, the dearest of people. Poor Moozie. He was a tortured child, yet he brought boundless happiness to the hearts of my husband and me. After that painful business and his leaving London, I lost touch with him, and though I made every effort to re-establish contact I failed. Poor Moozie. What slightly lightens the pain of losing him is the knowledge that he spent the last years of his life happily amongst you and that he married a good wife and had two sons. Please give my love to Mrs Sa'eed. Let her think of me as a mother and if there's anything I

147

can do for her and her two dear children, tell her not to hesitate to write to me. How happy I'd be if they all came and spent the next summer holidays with me. I am living here alone in the Isle of Wight. Last January I travelled to Cairo and visited my husband's grave. Ricky had a great love for Cairo and fate decreed that he should be buried in the city he loved more than any other in the world.

'I am keeping myself busy writing a book about our life – about Ricky, Moozie and me. They were both great men, each in his own way. Ricky's greatness lay in his ability to bring happiness to others. He was somebody who was happy in the real sense of the word; he exuded happiness to everyone he came into contact with. Moozie had the mind of a genius, but he was unstable; he was incapable of either accepting or giving happiness other than to those he really loved and was loved by, like Ricky and me. I feel that love and duty require me to tell people the story of those two great men. The book will actually be about Ricky and Moozie because I did nothing of note. I shall write of the splendid services Ricky rendered to Arabic culture, such as his discovery of so many rare manuscripts, the commentaries he wrote on them, and the way he supervised the printing of them. I shall write about the great part played by Moozie in drawing attention here to the misery in which his countrymen live under our colonial mandate, and I shall write in detail about the trial and shall clear his name of all suspicion. I shall be grateful if you'd send me anything left behind by

Moozie which would be of assistance to me in writing this book. Perhaps Moozie told you he'd made me trustee of his affairs in London. A certain amount of money has accumulated from royalties from some of his books and from translation rights on others, which I shall forward on directly you let me have the address of the bank to which you want me to transfer it. In this connection let me thank you very much for accepting to look after dear Moozie's family. Please write to me regularly and tell me their news, also send me a photo of them in your next letter.

Yours sincerely,
Elizabeth.'

I placed the letter in my pocket and seated myself in the chair to the right of the fireplace. My glance fell on an issue of *The Times* dated Monday 26 September 1927. Births, Marriages, Deaths. The marriage was conducted by the Rev. Canon Sampson M.A. Funeral service at Stuntney Church, 2 o'clock Wednesday. The Personal Column: Ever beloved. Will it be much longer? 'Dear Heart.' Kenya Colony – Mr. . . . . . . Chartered Surveyor returns to Nairobi October 5th. Until then communications regarding reports on properties in the Colony should be addressed to him care of . . . . Advertisement for riding lessons. Blue Persian cats for sale. Girl (17), refined, of gentle birth, seeks opening. Lady by birth (30) desires post abroad. Sports news: West Hill beat Burhill. West Ham Win. The Victory of Gene Tunney. A letter from Zafrullah Khan in which he refutes the views of Sir Chimanlal Setalvad about the dispute between the Moslems and the Hindus in the Punjab. A letter saying that jazz is a cheerful music in a sunless world. Two elephants from Rangoon arrived at the Zoo yesterday, having walked from Tilbury Docks. Cattle breeder was attacked by a bull on his farm and gored to death. A man who stole four bananas was sentenced to three years' penal servitude. Imperial and Foreign News. The New offer from Moscow to settle the Russian debt to France. Floods in Switzerland. *The Discovery*, Captain Scott's ship, has returned from the Southern Seas. Herr Stresemann gave a speech on disarmament in Geneva on Saturday. Herr Stresemann also made a statement to the 'Matin' paper in which he supported President Von Hindenburg's speech at Tannenberg in which he denied that Germany was responsible for the outbreak of the war. The leading article was about the Treaty of Jeddah which was signed by Sir Gilbert Clayton on behalf of Great Britain and Prince Feisal Abdul-Aziz Al Saud on behalf of his father, the King of the Hejaz and of Nejd and its dependencies. Weather Forecast for England and Wales: Winds mainly between W. and N.W., strong at times in exposed places; considerable fair intervals, but a few thundery showers and perhaps occasional local rains.

It appeared to be the only newspaper. Was there any significance in its presence here or was it here by mere chance?

Opening a notebook, I read on the first page: 'My Life Story – by Mustafa Sa'eed.' On the next page was the dedication: 'To those who see with one eye, speak with one tongue and see things as either black or white, either Eastern or Western.' I flicked through the rest of the pages but found nothing – not a single sentence, not a single word. Did this too have some significance or was it mere chance? I opened a file and found numerous papers, sketches and drawings. He was, it seems, trying his hand at writing and drawing. The drawings were good and revealed real talent. Coloured drawings of English country scenes in which oak trees, rivers and swans were repeated; pencil sketches of scenes and people from our village. Despite everything I cannot but admit his great skill. Bakri, Mahjoub, my grandfather, Wad Rayyes, Hosna, my uncle Abdul Karim, and others: their faces looked out at me with the penetrating expressions I had long been aware of but which I had been incapable of defining. Mustafa Sa'eed had drawn them with a clarity of vision and sympathy that approached love. Wad Rayyes's face was more in evidence than the others – eight drawings of him in different poses. Why was he so interested in Wad Rayyes?

I looked at some scraps of paper and read, 'We teach people in order to open up their minds and release their captive powers. But we cannot predict the result. Freedom – we free their minds from superstition. We give the people the keys of the future to act therein as they wish.' 'I left London with Europe having begun to mobilize her armies once again for even more ferocious violence.' 'It was not hatred. It was a love unable to express itself. I loved her in a twisted manner. She too.' 'The roofs of the houses are all wettened by the drizzle. The cows and sheep in the fields are like white and black pebbles.

The light rain of June. Allow me, Madam. These tráin journeys are boring. How do you do? From Birmingham. To London. How do you describe the scenery? Trees and grass. Haystacks in the middle of the fields. The trees and the grass are the same everywhere. A book by Ngaio Marsh. She hesitated. She didn't say yes or no.' Was he describing real events or plotting out a story? 'My lord, I must object to the prosecution's resorting to a clear dialectical trick in that he wants to establish the accused's responsibility for events for which he was not responsible, basing his argument upon something that did in fact happen; he then confirms his assumption of what happened on the basis of his previous assumptions. The accused admits he killed his wife, but this does not make him responsible for all the incidents of suicide by women in the British Isles during the past ten years.' 'He who breeds good, for him are hatched young birds that fly with happiness. He who breeds evil, for him there grows a tree whose thorns are sorrow and whose fruit is regret. May God have mercy on someone who has turned a blind eye to error and has indulged in the outward aspect of things.'

I found as well a poem in his handwriting. It seems he was also dabbling in poetry, and it was clear from all the crossings-out and changes that he too was somewhat awed when face to face with art. Here it is:

The sighs of the unhappy in the breast do groan
The vicissitudes of Time by silent tears are shown
And love and buried hate the winds away have blown.

Deep silence has embraced the vestiges of prayer,
Of moans and supplications and cries of woeful care,
And dust and smoke the traveller's path ensnare.

Some, souls content, others in dismay.
Brows submissive, others . . .

Mustafa Sa'eed had no doubt spent long hours searching for the right word to fit the metre. The problem intrigued me and I gave it several minutes' thought. I did not, though, waste too much time on it, for in any case it is a very poor poem that relies on antithesis and comparisons; it has no true feeling, no genuine emotion. This line of mine is no worse than the rest, so I crossed out the last line of the poem and wrote in its place:

Heads humbly bent and faces turned away.

I went on rummaging among the papers and found some scraps on which had been written such phrases as 'Three barrels of oil', 'The Committee will discuss the question of strengthening the base for the pump', and 'The surplus cement can be sold immediately'. Then I found this passage: 'It was inevitable that my star of destiny should come into collision with hers and that I should spend years in prison and yet more years roaming the face of the earth chasing her phantom and being chased by it. The sensation that, in an instant outside the bounds of time, I have bedded the goddess of Death and gazed out upon Hell from the aperture of her eyes – it's a feeling no man can imagine. The taste of that night stays on in my mouth, preventing me from savouring anything else.'

I became bored with reading the bits of paper. No doubt there were many more bits buried away in this room, like pieces in an arithmetical puzzle, which Mustafa Sa'eed wanted me to discover and to place side by side and so come out with a composite picture which would reflect favourably upon him. He wants to be discovered, like some historical object of value. There was no doubt of that, and I now know that it was me he had chosen for that role. It was no coincidence that he had excited my curiosity and had then told me his life story incompletely so that I myself might unearth the rest of it. It was no coincidence that he had left me a letter sealed with red wax to further sharpen my curiosity, and that he had made me guardian of his two sons so as to commit me irrevocably, and that he had left me the key to this wax museum. There was no limit to his egoism and his conceit; despite everything, he wanted history to immortalize him. But I do not have the time to proceed further with this farce. I must end it before the break of dawn and the time now was after two in the morning. At the break of dawn tongues of fire will devour these lies.

Jumping to my feet, I raised the candlelight to the oil painting on the mantelpiece. Everything in the room was neatly in its place – except for Jean Morris's picture. It was as if he had not known what to do with it. Though he had kept photographs of all the other women, Jean Morris was there as he saw her, not as seen by the camera. I looked admiringly at the picture. It was the long face of a woman with wide eyes and brows that joined up above them; the nose was on the large size, the mouth slightly too wide. The expression on the face is difficult to put into words: a disturbing, puzzling expression. The thin lips were tightly closed as though she were grinding her teeth, while her jaw was thrust forward haughtily. Was the expression in the eyes anger or a smile? There was something sensual that hovered round the whole face. Was this, then, the phoenix that had ravished the ghoul? That night his voice had been wounded, sad, tinged with regret. Was it because he had lost her? Or was it because she had made him swallow such degradations?

'I used to find her at every party I went to, as though she made a point of being where I was in order to humiliate me. When I wanted to dance with her, she would say, "I wouldn't dance with you if you were the only man in the world." When I slapped her cheek, she kicked me and bit into my arm with teeth like those of a lioness. She did no work and I don't know how she managed to live. Her family were from Leeds; I never met them, not even after I married her, and I know nothing about them except for the odd bits she used to tell me. Her father was a merchant, though I don't know of what. According to her she was the only girl among five brothers. She used to lie about the most ordinary things and would return home with amazing and incredible stories about incidents that had happened to her and people she'd met. I wouldn't be surprised if she didn't have a family at all and was like some mendicant Scheherazade. However, she was exceedingly intelligent, and exceedingly charming when she wanted to be, and wherever she went she was surrounded by a band of admirers buzzing round her like flies. Deep within me I felt that, despite her show of disliking me, I interested her; when she and I were brought together at some gathering, she would watch me out of the corner of her eye, taking note of everything I did and said, and if she saw me showing any interest in another woman she was quick to be unpleasant to her. Brazen in word and deed, she abstained from nothing – stealing, lying and cheating; yet, against my will, I fell in love with her and I was no longer able to control the course of events. When I avoided her she would entice me to her, and when I ran after her she fled from me. Once, taking hold of myself, I kept away from her for two weeks. I began to avoid the places she frequented and if I was invited to a party I made sure before going that she wouldn't be there. Nevertheless, she found her way to my house and surprised me late one Saturday night when Ann Hammond was with me. She heaped filthy curses upon Ann Hammond, and when I tried to drive her away with blows she was not deterred. Ann Hammond left in tears, while she stayed on, standing in front of me like some demon, a challenging defiance in her eyes that stirred remote longings in my heart. Without our exchanging a word, she stripped off her clothes and stood naked before me. All the fires of hell blazed within my breast. Those fires had to be extinguished in that mountain of ice that stood in my path. As I advanced towards her, my limbs trembling, she pointed to an expensive Wedgwood vase on the mantelpiece. "Give this to me and you can have me," she said. If she had asked at that moment for my life as a price I would have paid it. I nodded my head in agreement. Taking up the vase, she smashed it on the ground and began trampling the pieces underfoot. She pointed to a rare Arabic manuscript on the table. "Give me this too," she said. My throat grew dry with a thirst that almost killed me. I must quench it with a drink of icy water. I nodded my head in agreement. Taking up the old, rare manuscript she tore it to bits, filling her mouth with pieces of paper which she chewed and spat out. It was as though she had chewed at my very liver. And yet I didn't care. She pointed to a silken Isphahan prayer-rug which I had been given by Mrs Robinson when I left Cairo. It was the most valuable thing I owned, the thing I treasured most. "Give me this too and then you can have me," she said. Hesitating for a moment, I glanced at her as she stood before me, erect and lithe, her eyes agleam with a dangerous brightness, her lips like a forbidden fruit that must be eaten. I nodded my head in agreement. Taking up the prayer-rug, she threw it on to the fire and stood watching gloatingly as it was consumed, the flames reflected on her face. This woman is my quarry and I shall follow her to Hell. I walked up to her and, placing my arm round her waist, leaned over to kiss her. Suddenly I felt a violent jab from her knee between my thighs. When I regained consciousness I found she had disappeared.

'I continued in pursuit of her for three years. My caravans were thirsty, and the mirage shimmered before me in the wilderness of longing. "You're a savage bull that does not weary of the chase," she said to me one day. "I am tired of your pursuing me and of my running before you. Marry me." I married her at the Registry Office in Fulham, no one else attending except for a girl-friend of hers and a friend of mine. As she repeated after the Registrar "I Jean Winifred Morris accept this man Mustafa Sa'eed Othman as my lawfully wedded husband, for better and for worse, for richer for poorer, in sickness and in health . . ." she suddenly burst into violent sobbing. I was amazed at her expressing such emotion and the Registrar stopped the ceremony and said to her kindly, "Come, come. I can understand how you feel. Just a few more moments and it'll all be over." After which she continued to whimper, and when it was over she once again broke out sobbing. The Registrar went up and patted her on the shoulder, then shook me by the hand, saying, "Your wife is crying because she's so happy. I have seen many women cry at their marriage, but I've never seen such violent weeping. It seems she loves you very much. Look after her. I'm sure you'll both be happy.' She went on crying till we had left the Registry Office, when suddenly her tears turned to laughter. "What a farce!" she said, guffawing with laughter.

'We spent the remainder of the day drinking. No party, no guests – just she and I and drink. When night brought us together in bed, I wanted to possess her. "Not now," she said, turning her back on me. "I'm tired." For two months she wouldn't let me near her; every night she would say "I'm tired" or "I'm unwell." No longer capable of taking any more, one night I stood over her with a knife in my hand. "I'll kill you," I told her. She glanced at the knife with what seemed to me like longing. "Here's my breast bared to you," she said. "Plunge the knife in." I looked at her naked body which, though within my grasp, I did not possess. Sitting on the side of the bed, I bowed my head meekly. She placed her hand on my cheek and said in a tone that was not devoid of gentleness: "My sweet, you're not the kind of man that kills." I experienced a feeling of ignominy, loneliness, and loss. Suddenly I remembered my mother. I saw her face clearly in my mind's eye and heard her saying to me "It's your life and you're free to do with it as you will." I remembered that the news of my mother's death had reached me nine months ago and had found me drunk and in the arms of a woman. I don't recollect now which woman it was; I do, though, recollect that I felt no sadness – it was as though the matter was of absolutely no concern to me. I remembered this and wept from deep within my heart. I wept so much I thought I would never stop. I felt Jean embracing me and saying things I couldn't make out, though her voice was repellent to me and sent a shudder through my body. I pushed her violently from me. "I hate you," I shouted at her. "I swear I'll kill you one day." In the throes of my sorrow the expression in her eyes did not escape me. They shone brightly and gave me a strange look. Was it surprise? Was it fear? Was it desire? Then, in a voice of simulated tenderness, she said: "I too, my sweet, hate you. I shall hate you until death."

'But there was nothing I could do. Having been a hunter, I had become the quarry. I was in torment; and, in a way I could not understand, I derived pleasure from my suffering. Exactly eleven days after that incident – I remember it because I had

159

swallowed its agonies as the man fasting swallows the agonies of the month of Ramadan when it falls in the scorching heat of summer – we were in Richmond Park just before sunset. The park was not wholly empty of people; we heard voices and saw figures moving in the evening glow. We talked only a little and exchanged no expressions of love or flirtation. Without reason she put her arms round my neck and gave me a long kiss. I felt her breast pressing against me. Putting my arms round her waist I pulled her to me and she moaned in a way that tore at my heart-strings and made me oblivious of everything. I no longer remembered anything; I no longer saw or was conscious of anything but this catastrophe, in the shape of a woman, that fate had decreed for me. She was my destiny and in her lay my destruction, yet for me the whole world was not worth a mustard seed in comparison. I was the invader who had come from the South, and this was the icy battlefield from which I would not make a safe return. I was the pirate sailor and Jean Morris the shore of destruction. And yet I did not care. I took her, there in the open air, unconcerned whether we could be seen or heard by people. For me this moment of ecstasy is worth the whole of life.

'The moments of ecstasy were in fact rare; the rest of the time we spent in a murderous war in which no quarter was given. The war invariably ended in my defeat. When I slapped her, she would slap me back and dig her nails into my face; a volcano of violence would explode within her and she would break any crockery that came to hand and tear up books and papers. This was the most dangerous weapon she had and every battle would end with her ripping up an important book or burning some piece of research on which I had worked for weeks on end. Sometimes I would be so overcome with rage that I would reach the brink of madness and murder and would tighten my grip on her throat, when she would suddenly grow quiet and give me that enigmatic look, a mixture of astonishment, fear, and desire. Had I exerted just that little bit more pressure I would have put an end to the war. Sometimes the war would take us out. Once in a pub she suddenly shouted, "That son of a bitch is making passes at me." I sprang at the man and we seized each other by the throat. People collected round us and suddenly behind me I heard her guffawing with laughter. One of the men who had come to separate us said to me, "I'm sorry to have to tell you, if this woman's your wife, you've married a whore." He didn't say a word to her. "It seems this woman enjoys making violent scenes." My anger transferred itself to her and while she was still guffawing with laughter I went up to her. I slapped her and in her usual way she plunged her nails into my face. Only after a lot of trouble was I able to drag her off home.

'She used to like flirting with every Tom, Dick and Harry whenever we went out together. She would flirt with waiters in restaurants, bus conductors and passers-by. Some would take courage and respond while others would answer with obscene remarks, and so I'd get myself into fights with people, and exchange blows with her in the middle of the street. How often have I asked myself what it was that bound me to her! Why didn't I leave her and escape? But I knew there was nothing I could do about it and that the tragedy had to happen. I knew she was being unfaithful to me; the whole house was impregnated with the smell of infidelity. Once I found a man's handkerchief which wasn't mine. "It's yours," she said when I asked her. "This handkerchief isn't mine," I told her. "Assuming it's not your handkerchief," she said, "what are you going to do about it?" On another occasion I found a cigarette case, then a pen. "You're being unfaithful to me," I said to her. "Suppose I am being unfaithful to you," she said. "I swear I'll kill you," I shouted at her. "You only say that," she said with a jeering smile. "What's stopping you from killing me? What are you waiting for? Perhaps you're waiting till you find a man lying on top of me, and even then I don't think you'd do anything. You'd sit on the edge of the bed and cry."

'It was a dark evening in February, the temperature ten degrees below zero. Evening was like morning, morning like night – dark and gloomy. The sun had not shone for twenty-two days. The whole city was a field of ice – ice in the streets and in the front gardens of the houses. The water froze in the pipes and people's breath came out from their mouths like steam. The trees were bare, their branches collapsing under the weight of snow. And all the while my blood was boiling and my head in a fever. On a night such as this momentous deeds occur. This was the night of reckoning. I walked from the station to the house carrying my overcoat over my arm, for my body was burning hot and the sweat poured from my forehead. Though ice crackled under my shoes, yet I sought the cold. Where was the cold? I found her stretched out naked on the bed, her white thighs open. Though her lips were formed into a full smile, there was something like sadness on her face; it was as though she was in a state of great readiness both to give and to take. On first seeing her my heart was filled with tenderness and I felt that Satanic warmth under the diaphragm which tells me that I am in control of the situation. Where had this warmth been all these years? "Was anyone with you?" I said to her in a confident voice I thought I had lost for ever. "There was no one with me," she answered me in a voice affected by the impact of mine. "This night is for you alone. I've been waiting for you a long time." I felt that for the first time she was telling me the truth. This night was to be the night of truth and of tragedy. I removed the knife from its sheath and sat on the edge of the bed for a time looking at her. I saw the impact of my glances live and palpable on her face. We looked into each other's eyes, and as our glances met and joined it was though we were two celestial bodies that had merged in an ill-omened moment of time. My glances overwhelmed her and she turned her face from me, but the effect was apparent in the area below her waist which she shifted from right to left, raising herself slightly off the bed; then she settled down, her arms thrown out languorously, and resumed looking at me. I looked at her breast and she too looked at where my glance had fallen, as though she had been robbed of her own volition and was moving in accordance with my will. I looked at her stomach and as she followed my gaze a faint expression of pain came over her face. As my gaze lingered, so did hers; when I hurried she hurried with me. I looked long at her white, wide-open thighs, as though massaging them with my eyes, and my gaze slipped from the soft, smooth surface till it came to rest there, in the repository of secrets, where good and evil are born. I saw a blush spread up her face and her eyelids droop as though she had been unable to control them. Slowly I raised the dagger and she followed the blade with her eyes; the pupils widened suddenly and her face shone with a fleeting light like a flash of lightning. She continued to look at the blade-edge with a mixture of astonishment, fear, and lust. Then she took hold of the dagger and kissed it fervently. Suddenly she closed her eyes and stretched out in the bed, raising her middle slightly, opening her thighs wider. "Please, my sweet," she said, moaning: "Come – I'm ready now." When I did not answer her appeal she gave a more agonizing moan. She waited. She wept. Her voice was so faint it could hardly be heard. "Please darling."

'Here are my ships, my darling, sailing towards the shores of destruction. I leant over and kissed her. I put the blade-edge between her breasts and she twined her legs round my back. Slowly I pressed down. Slowly. She opened her eyes. What ecstasy there was in those eyes! She seemed more beautiful than anything in the whole world. "Darling," she said painfully, "I thought you would never do this. I almost gave up hope of you." I pressed down the dagger with my chest until it had all disappeared between her breasts. I could feel the hot blood gushing from her chest. I began crushing my chest against her as she called out imploringly: "Come with me. Come with me. Don't let me go alone."

'"I love you," she said to me, and I believed her. "I love you," I said to her, and I spoke the truth. We were a torch of flame, the edges of the bed tongues of Hell-fire. The smell of smoke was in my nostrils as she said to me "I love you, my darling," and as I said to her "I love you, my darling," and the universe, with its past, present and future, was gathered together into a single point before and after which nothing existed.'

I entered the water as naked as when my mother bore me. When I first touched the cold water I felt a shudder go through me, then the shudder was transformed into a sensation of wakefulness. The river was not in full spate as during the days of the flooding nor yet was it at its lowest level. I had put out the candles and locked the door of the room and that of the courtyard without doing anything. Another fire would not have done any good. I left him talking and went out. I did not let him complete the story. I thought of going and standing by her grave. I thought of throwing away the key where nobody could find it. Then I decided against it. Meaningless acts. Yet I had to do something. My feet led me to the river bank as the first glimmerings of dawn made their appearance in the east. I would dispel my rage by swimming. The objects on the two shores were half visible, appearing and disappearing, veering between light and darkness. The river was reverberating with its old familiar voice, moving yet having the appearace of being still. There was no sound except for the reverberation of the river and the puttering of the water-pump not far away. I began swimming towards the northern shore. I went on swimming and swimming till the movements of my body settled down into restful harmony with the forces of the river. I was no longer thinking as I moved forward through the water. The impact of my arms as they struck the water, the movement of my legs, the sound of my heavy breathing, the reverberation of the river and the noise of the pump puttering on the shore – these were the only noises. I continued swimming and swimming, resolved to make the northern shore. That was the goal. In front of me the shore rose and fell, the noises being totally cut off and then blaring forth. Little by little I came to hear nothing but the reverberation of the river. Then it was as if I were in a vast echoing hall. The shore rose and fell. The reverberation of the river faded and overflowed. In front of me I saw things in a semicircle. Then I veered between seeing and blindness. I was conscious and not conscious. Was I asleep or awake? Was I alive or dead? Even so, I was still holding a thin, frail thread: the feeling that the goal was in front of me, not below me, and that I must move forwards and not downwards. But the thread was so frail it almost snapped and I reached a point where I felt that the forces lying in the river-bed were pulling me down to them. A numbness ran through my legs and arms. The hall expanded and the answering echoes quickened. Now – and suddenly, with a force that came to me from I know not where – I raised my body in the water. I heard the reverberation of the river and the puttering of the water pump. Turning to left and right, I found I was half-way between north and south. I was unable to continue, unable to return. I turned over on to my back and stayed there motionless, with difficulty moving my arms and legs as much as was needed to keep me afloat. I was conscious of the river's destructive forces pulling me downwards and of the current pushing me to the southern shore in a curving angle. I would not be able to keep thus poised for long; sooner or later the river's forces would pull me down into its depths. In a state between life and death I saw formations of sand grouse heading northwards. Were we in winter or summer? Was it a casual flight or a migration? I felt myself submitting to the destructive forces of the river, felt my legs dragging the rest of my body downwards. In an instant – I know not how long or short it was – the reverberation of the river turned into a piercingly loud roar and at the very same instant there was a vivid brightness like a flash of lightning. Then, for an indeterminate period, quiet and darkness reigned, after which I became aware of the sky moving away and drawing close, the shore rising and falling. Suddenly I experienced a violent desire for a cigarette. It wasn't merely a desire; it was a hunger, a thirst. And this was the instant of waking from the nightmare. The sky settled into place, as did the bank, and I heard the puttering of the pump and was aware of the coldness of the water on my body. Then my mind cleared and my relationship to the river was determined. Though floating on the water, I was not part of it. I thought that if I died at that moment, I would have died as I was born – without any volition of mine. All my life I had not chosen, had not decided. Now I am making a decision. I choose life. I shall live because there are a few people I want to stay with for the longest possible time and because I have duties to discharge. It is not my concern whether or not life has meaning. If I am unable to forgive, then I shall try to forget. I shall live by force and cunning. I moved my feet and arms, violently and with difficulty, until the upper part of my body was above water. Like a comic actor shouting on a stage, I screamed with all my remaining strength, 'Help! Help!'